Banish Stress and Pain

'Relaxation and massage for every body'

Combat the tension and aches
of day to day living.
Every body can learn
and benefit from these easy exercises
and massage routines.

WISEBUY PUBLICATIONS

Other books from Wisebuy Publications

Healthy Eating £3.95
Allergy? Think About Food £2.95
Crying Baby How To Cope £3.50
The Savers & Investors Guide £4.50
Shares – A Beginner's Guide to Making Money £2.95

Available from Wisebuy Publications
25 West Cottages London NW6 1RJ
plus 50p p&p for each book ordered.
Or ask at your bookshop.

Banish Stress and Pain

Ross Valentine

Drawings by Larry Wakefield

Edited by Susan Lewis

WISEBUY PUBLICATIONS

First published 1990

Copyright © 1990 Ross Valentine

**Further copies of BANISH STRESS AND
PAIN can be obtained from Wisebuy
Publications, 25 West Cottages, London NW6
1RJ, price £4.95 plus 50p p+p (UK) or £7
airmail including p+p.**

While great care had been taken to ensure that
the information in this book was correct at the
time of publication, the author and publishers
cannot accept legal liability for any errors or
omissions, nor can they accept responsibility with
regard to the standing of any organisation
mentioned in the text, nor any injury sustained
by a reader disregarding or misinterpreting the
instructions given in the text.

**British Library Cataloguing in Publication
Data**
Valentine Ross
    Banish stress and pain : relaxation and
    massage for every body.
    1. Physical fitness. Massage – Manuals
    I. Title
    613.7'9

    ISBN 0-9514595-0-3

*Typesetting by MC Typeset Ltd.,
Gillingham, Kent
Printed by The Guernsey Press Ltd*

Contents

her back. Swollen wrists and hands. Stroking her forearm. Kneading her forearm. Neck and head aches.

List of drawings

Acknowledgements

I would like to thank my friends who read through the draft of the book, Peter Francis who kept my word processor working, and Susan Lewis for her firm but thoughtful editing. Special thanks are due to Larry Wakefield for his excellent drawings, to Popi MacFarlane for modelling for the drawings, and to Lesley Hobbs for her advice and guidance on the pregnancy chapter.

Above all I must thank the people who have attended my massage and relaxation classes. Teaching them taught me what they needed to know and made this book possible.

Last but not least my thanks go to my family for their tolerance of the hours spent on this book away from them.

The author

Ross Valentine has taught relaxation and massage for many years, both at adult education classes and privately. His pupils have come from all walks of life and include business men and women, doctors, nurses, manual workers, housewives, electricians and tree surgeons.

An osteopath and acupuncturist, he has been in practice for eleven years and run his own practice for the last eight years. He is married with three young children and is a keen sailor and French Horn player. He lives in Southampton.

The artist

Larry Wakefield is an artist who has exhibited widely in this country and in Europe. His work is permanently displayed at the Warwick Arts Trust, Southampton and Portsmouth City Art Galleries, and in numerous private and public collections.

His illustrations, which are largely related to figurative and architectural subjects, are a natural extension to the imagery in his paintings. He lives and works in Southampton.

1
Stress and strain

That wretched headache which grips you at the back of the neck and ends up spreading all over your head, making the rest of your day a misery. A bad back after a stint in the garden or a day at work. Start-of-season aches at the local sports or football club. Aching shoulder muscles after a drive in traffic or on the motorway. Or plain tiredness after a long day with the children or at the office.

The stress and strain which constantly bombard your body and mind are part of everyday life. Individually they may seem small, even trivial, but collectively they amount to considerable pressure.

The factory worker is subjected to loud noises in his workshop or production line. The woman on the electronics assembly line must concentrate for long periods on her task. Draughtsmen bend over drawings for hours on end while salesmen and women struggle to sell products to achieve their targets. Managers have the continuing worries of running their departments, and self-employed people have their own business worries without the security of a big firm and regular pay cheques behind them.

The harassed housewife may have to cope with small children and a part time job as well while she or her husband must take on the worries of family finance, the mortgage and saving towards a holiday or new car.

How do you deal with this daily bag of troubles? When you are properly ill your doctor can help. But when you feel tense or achey or plain tired there is usually little your GP can offer. You are thrown back onto your own resources. Lots of people put up with it and suffer. You don't have to.

Muscular tension

One of the most common effects of stress is muscular tension in your neck and shoulders. Your shoulders feel tight and stiff and usually ache as well. Sometimes the ache spreads further down your back and up your neck. You may experience the same physical tension elsewhere. Tight jaw muscles often result from tension. Headaches can come from tight neck muscles while back ache may be caused by holding yourself rigid. Any muscle held tight for a prolonged period will hurt.

Illness

Stress is a significant cause of much illness and disease. In some cases it is the principal cause. Serious effects of prolonged stress include insomnia, high blood pressure, heart disease, ulcers, bowel problems, asthma, reduced fertility, menstrual problems, allergies, and reduced resistance to infection. Some cancers may also be linked to stress.

Physical symptoms may include cold sweaty hands, nausea, butterflies in the stomach, dry mouth and palpitations.

There are also the mental symptoms of stress. Your ability to concentrate can be impaired: you find yourself getting forgetful or having mental blocks. Emotions are also affected. You suffer feelings of helplessness, depression, loneliness or panic. You may feel frustration, fear, anxiety and fright. Your behaviour may change. You freeze and become clumsy. Often people start to drink or smoke heavily. Some chew their finger nails or develop other nervous habits. These problems may be related to stress and your doctor should tell you if stress is involved.

Help yourself

Many people visit osteopaths, chiropractors, masseurs or physiotherapists to relieve aches and pains caused by muscular tension and stress. However there is often no need to seek professional help since these problems can frequently be helped with some simple relaxation or massage at home.

This book deals with the relief of muscular tension, aches, pain and stress through relaxation, deep breathing exercises and massage. Since tension is so often associated with some sort of emotional stress, physical relaxation can have benefits far beyond those of easing tightened knotted muscles. It can calm your entire being.

2
Coping with stress

Everyone is subject to stress from time to time. It happens when you feel you cannot meet the demands being made on you.

Suppose you are asked to perform a task. Your stress level will depend on whether you feel you can do it. If you are confident you can, the stress will be low. If you think you cannot it will be higher. It is not your ability to do the job that is relevant but whether you *think* you can do it. A friend or colleague may tell you that you will find it easy and you have all the skill and knowledge required. But if you continue to doubt your ability to do the task you will find yourself experiencing stress.

Since humans have great powers of imagination you can produce stress by imagining a situation that you would not be able to cope with. This is where a lot of worrying comes from. A lot of things you worry about never come about. You worry that the mortgage rate might go up and you will not be able to afford the extra payments. You worry that you will not be able to pass an exam when in fact you do. You may worry that you will not get on with a colleague or an in-law. In the end a lot of these events either do not occur, or when they do occur you cope with them perfectly well. However, the anticipation of your inability to cope has produced stress.

Modern lifestyles

For better or worse you live in the twentieth century which involves a complex lifestyle with many conflicting demands. Besides the simple age-old demands for food and warmth, companionship, shelter, help in illness and bereavement, there are the more modern demands of time schedules, deadlines to meet, contracts to fulfil.

Then there are the demands due to expectation. These come from others as well as yourself: keeping up with the Joneses, the self-fuelling fire of need for a hi-fi, television, and the latest model of motor car.

There are the demands of work, the boredom of some jobs, the tremendous pressure of others, the hopes for promotion and the elation or disappointment when these hopes are or are not fulfilled.

There is the very pace of life itself. Travel to far away places takes hours when only two generations ago it would have taken weeks. You have to adjust to new climates and cultures very quickly. News and information reach you rapidly from all over the world coming in great quantities. The very speed of communication requires you to react swiftly.

Fight or flight

Stress is a reaction of the body and mind. There is within everyone an instinctive mechanism for reacting to a situation which is dangerous. It is called the fight or flight reaction because it enables you to do either of those things: fight or flee. Since humans first appeared on earth physical danger has always been present but your body has a very efficient means of reacting to it by switching on automatically when danger is perceived.

In your brain there is a small area, the hypothalamus, which controls the hormonal glands of the body. When a danger is spotted the hypothalamus is immediately alerted. It sets in motion a series of reactions which rapidly prepare your body for physical action. Priority is given to functions and organs which will be of immediate use in saving your life. Your muscles are going to have to work very hard, so blood being used for digestion is diverted to the muscles, and digestion slows down. Your muscles will use a lot of energy, so the heart pumps faster and stronger to get vital oxygen to them as quickly as possible. As a result, not only does your heart rate increase but your blood pressure rises as well. In order that the demand for increased oxygen can be met and the increased quantities of carbon dioxide produced by the hard working muscles removed, your breathing alters.

Other changes take place too. You start to sweat more so that the heat which is expected to be produced in the coming physical action can be got rid of. Your energy reserves in the liver are mobilised to supply the muscles. The mechanism in your body which deals with infections is suppressed and various changes in the composition of the blood take place. The adrenal glands produce adrenaline which sustains this reaction.

All this takes place very quickly. When physical action has taken place and the crisis has been dealt with, the various biochemicals produced will have been used up. You then revert to normal and everything carries on as before.

For most animals, and man is one species of animal, threats are usually physical and therefore a physical response is needed. However, for twentieth century western man the majority of threats are not physical and therefore a physical response is of no use.

Imagine you are at the traffic lights and your engine stalls. The cars behind you start blowing their horns. Or you are stuck behind a car that has stalled and you have a train to catch. Perhaps a car has just cut across you without signalling. Apart from feeling annoyed or angry, your body reacts by invoking the fight or flight response. However these situations do not require a physical response. The reaction is no use in resolving things and your various bodily changes are not needed.

It is clear that such a response, though at times vital for your very survival, is often invoked unnecessarily. If this happens occasionally no harm is done but when these reactions take place daily your body is going to suffer.

A little pressure

You need a certain amount of pressure in order to function effectively. Too little pressure and demands can also be a source of stress. Necessity is not only the mother of invention, it is also the mother of action. The amount of pressure each person needs differs. You may love rock climbing and feel very bored living a quiet life. Your counterpart however may find suburban life totally satisfactory and the thought of rock climbing terrifying. You may thrive on public debate and discussions or you may freeze when asked to talk in front of a lot of people.

Too much is too much

As demands on you increase, your performance will also increase but only up to a certain point. When you reach that point, called the fatigue point, any further demand leads to a decrease in your performance. Jane Madders coined the phrase fatigue point in her book *Stress and Relaxation*. Look at Drawing 1 overleaf. The dotted line shows how you might assume or expect your performance to continue improving. In fact, having reached the fatigue point, your performance starts to decrease if the demand on you continues to increase. Eventually you get to a state of exhaustion. If this is ignored or neglected then illness or

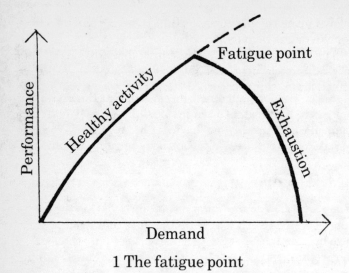

1 The fatigue point

some sort of breakdown is quite a possibility.

The part of the curve leading up to the fatigue point represents a state of healthy activity. You are coping fine here and can sustain this degree of demand or pressure for quite some time. You may be taking time off for rest and recreation as well so your general level of stress is kept at a reasonable level.

The trouble with going beyond the fatigue point is that you may not be aware that you have reached this stage. You think that you are not trying hard enough. The result is that more pressure is applied to try harder with no improvement; in fact, there is probably a fall in achievement leading to yet more pressure and therefore another fall in performance.

Ultimately, if nothing is done to break this vicious circle, it leads to exhaustion and possibly breakdown. Along the road you may start to behave badly with grumbling, bad temper and irritability. Small things get blown up out of all proportion and you may start to drink, smoke or eat heavily.

The fatigue point reflects the total level of demands and pressure made upon you. When you reach this point you must lower the pressure. If, for example, an especially high level of pressure is expected for a particular task, one solution is to reduce some of the other pressures you are under. Then all available energy can be concentrated on the main task. If you are studying for an important exam, preparing a special document for work or need to cope with an ill relative, other people in the house should take over your share of household duties until the pressure is finished.

Another way to reduce your overall level of pressure and stress is to take more time off for sport and recreation. You should also practise deep breathing and relaxation. Chapters 3 and 4 describe various methods to help you do this.

Everyone has a unique capacity for tolerating stress. There will always be people around who can be seen to have a greater capacity for handling pressure than you. With a certain amount of self study and reflection you can get some idea of how much pressure you can handle before the fatigue point is reached. However when it is reached the pressure must be reduced.

Know yourself

Examine your life and lifestyle to determine where the stress-arousing demands are coming from. Make a list of the demands made upon you. Include things you think or worry about as well as things you do. Give each item a score between 0 and 10 depending how stressful it is. The most stressful will have 10 against it. Read through this list. It will show you where a lot of your stress demands come from.

You can also make out a time sheet listing all the things you do during the day against the times you do them. Then go through the list marking the satisfying ones in one colour and the unsatisfying ones in a contrasting colour. Some things have to be done but are you trying to fit too many into your day? Are the unsatisfying ones balanced by satisfying ones? Are you balancing your work with leisure activities? Do you have too little to do? Is boredom on your list too?

Changes in your lifestyle can be stressful too. The bigger the change the more stressful. Even changes for the better can be stressful such as moving to a new house. It is when a lot of these events come close together that stress problems are likely to arise. Read through this list of lifestyle changes and see how many apply to you:

● Death of someone close to you
● Divorce
● Ill health (yours or someone else's)
● Marriage
● Moving house
● Sexual problems
● Loss of your job. (Redundancy, retirement, dismissal.)
● New baby
● Parent(s) come to live with you
● Changes at work
● Changes at home

Learn to say no

Everyone has obligations which have to be fulfilled. However there are many commitments people undertake unnecessarily. If you are feeling under pressure, one simple remedy is to say no. You may have to be tactful. Saying no in an aggressive way is likely to raise stress levels all round.

If an elderly relative is taking you for granted, refusing

point blank to take him or her shopping for the fourth
time that week might be too blunt. You may have to tell a
white lie, say a friend is coming to visit you, or you have to
go out.

Enlist the help of your spouse, especially if a child is
constantly asking for a treat or toy. Two people saying no
is easier than one.

At work your boss may not be aware that you have
enough on your plate at present. Just letting the work pile
up is going to increase your stress level. Tell him or her
that you have enough to cope with. Show how behind you
are. If he is not aware of the problem he is unlikely to do
anything about it. It may initially take a bit of courage to
say no but the next time it will be much easier. The
reduction in your load will more than compensate for the
temporary stress that saying no invoked.

Learn to say no to friends or relatives asking you to help
with their jumble sale, dig up their garden or walk their
dog. If you do not want to do it, say so.

Get used to it

A situation may be stressful because it only arises
occasionally. You are not sure about it or how well you can
cope. This uncertainty produces stress. One solution is to
face the problem more frequently so that you get used to
dealing with it.

For example, the first confrontation with computer
equipment or a new kitchen appliance can be quite
alarming. If you do not use it again for several weeks it
may still be intimidating. However, if you spend several
days in succession getting to grips with the machine, your
fears will be shown to be groundless and the problem
disappears. You will have gained the confidence to use the
machine without fear or stress.

Another example is driving in town. If you live in the

countryside, driving in a busy city can be a tense
experience at first. Some people find it terrifying. If you
only go into town occasionally you are likely to find your
visits remain stressful. However, if you drive in the city
regularly this nervousness can soon be replaced by
confidence as you learn to cope with the traffic.

Help others

Helping and listening to others can be an effective way of
coping with stress. Although your problems may seem
overwhelming to you, being in contact with other people
and their problems helps put yours into perspective. Often
your own problems lose their urgency when viewed
alongside the disadvantages under which others labour.

Hobbies and keeping fit

These are valuable ways of coping with stressful exist-
ences. Hobbies give people interests outside the pressing
run of daily problems. They help to keep your mind away
from worries, while at the same time provide absorbing
activities. The one track mind nature of worrying is often
self-sustaining and hobbies and interests can take your
mind off those rails. Keeping fit helps in a similar way.
Indeed sport is an important hobby in itself. Exercise
helps to work off accumulated tensions and fitness makes
stress easier to handle.

Change your environment

Sometimes you need to get away from a problem which is
causing trouble. This may mean a holiday, changing job,
home or even the area where you live. Of course this is not
necessarily practical and may just evade the issue with
the problem surfacing again later when you have moved.

It is, however, an option that needs to be considered.

Practise relaxation

A very important way of helping yourself cope with stress is the practice of physical relaxation. This reduces your level of physical tension and thereby helps lower mental tension as well. Another benefit of relaxation is increased self-awareness. Although most people acknowledge that their lives contain some stress, many are unaware of how tense and stressed they really are. It is only when you start to lower the stress levels that you begin to realise just how bad things had been. Chapter 4 describes the technique of relaxation.

Habits

Habit is a bad enemy but a very useful friend. Any action or thought carried out repeatedly eventually becomes a habit. This can be very difficult to change. With stress tension and worry become habits. Often you can help yourself by changing the way you view or respond to situations although expert counselling may sometimes be needed.

You can make relaxation a habit. Practise it regularly and frequently, preferably daily. Chapter 4 shows you how. As you practise you will realise how tense you used to be. This will give you a greater incentive to continue the habit of relaxation.

Fear of stress

One of the consequences of long-standing stress is that it can result in various symptoms being produced which are quite frightening. These include palpitations, knotted stomach, sweating and shaking hands. Unfortunately the fear these symptoms produce reinforces that stress, thus producing more of the same frightening symptoms. Two key elements in the management of this problem are:

● Face the symptoms. Do not hide from them in fear. A Chinese proverb says that a problem run away from turns into an elephant while one faced turns into a mouse.

● Accept the symptoms for what they are, just palpitations, sweaty hands or whatever, and nothing more. As they lose their threatening aspect the symptoms will start to diminish. The realisation that they are nothing to fear gives a great deal of relief.

3
Breathing

Shallow breathing is closely associated with tension while slow deep breathing is associated with relaxation or lack of tension. Breathing techniques are very useful for breaking the tension pattern and encouraging relaxation.

If you carry out a difficult or complicated task your breathing may become very shallow. Sometimes you might not breathe at all for a brief period. Afterwards your breathing becomes deeper again. Shallow breathing can do no harm over short periods. However it does lead to trouble when it becomes a habit.

When you are tense your breathing becomes shallow and often rapid. This is because you are preparing for physical action by invoking the emergency fight or flight reaction mentioned on page 17. There is a rapid intake of oxygen and an equally rapid removal of waste carbon dioxide from the blood. Although necessary in real emergencies this is no use when physical action is not needed: for example when you have an irate customer on the telephone, or when someone sounds his horn because you are late starting off at the traffic lights.

Keep control

Some muscles cannot be controlled by conscious decision. For example the muscles involved in digestion respond to the presence of food, not to your decision to digest. When you have eaten, the muscles automatically move the food through your digestive system without any instructions from you.

On the other hand, the muscles which make your body move are controlled by you. Suppose you want to lift something up. Your brain sends the appropriate messages along nerves to the muscles in your arms and hands. They then contract or relax as required. They do not work automatically. They need instructions from your brain. You have to initiate the motion deliberately.

Some muscles involved in breathing can be controlled by you although the way you use them is largely governed by habit. If your habit is to breathe shallowly then you will breathe shallowly even if it is inappropriate. Habits are very useful for helping actions to be performed repetitively without any conscious deliberation. However, if the action is bad or inappropriate the habit still persists until it is deliberately and consciously changed. Then new habits are formed which hopefully are better ones.

Breathing exercises

These have long been used to help relaxation and alleviate tension. Here are two simple but very effective ones. One teaches you how to control your breathing so that you can change it from shallow to deep at will. The other uses that control to help you breathe slowly and deeply. This relaxes you and releases tension.

Control exercise

This exercise helps you develop awareness and control of your depth of breathing. The term deeply does not mean taking in large volumes of air but rather that you breathe into the deeper or lower part of your lungs instead of into the top of your lungs. Some people have difficulty in doing breathing exercises at first because they find it hard to breathe deeply at will.

Lie on your back You should be comfortable with a pillow or cushion under your head. Lie on a bed or else on a carpet or rug. Do not lie on the bare floor because you will find its hardness uncomfortable. If it is a nice warm day lie outside on the grass.

Put both hands on your chest so that your finger tips are just touching. Lie there without doing anything. It does not matter whether you are breathing through your nose or your mouth. You do not need to take large breaths. Just breathe normally. Don't alter your breathing or press with your hands. Just lie there.

Close your eyes and note what your hands are doing. They should be gently rising and falling as you breathe in and out. As you breathe in your finger tips will part since your chest expands as air fills it up. As you breathe out your chest will lower as the air goes out and your finger tips will come together again.

Since you are at rest you will not be taking big breaths and the movements will be quite small. However they will be there. If you are not sure try taking one or two big breaths just to convince yourself that you can feel movement. Then let your breathing settle down to the normal resting rate it was a moment ago. Satisfy yourself that you can feel the movement quite clearly.

Move both your hands down so that they are resting on your abdomen a little above the navel. Again without doing anything, monitor any movement they are feeling.

Then move your hands up to the top of your chest so that they are just below the throat and again feel the movement.

You should have felt movement at all three levels of your chest but you might have felt more movement at one level than another. If you felt most movement low down over the abdomen then you were breathing deeply; if at the top then you were breathing shallowly.

Put one hand on the top of your chest below the throat. Put the other on your abdomen just above the navel and below your ribs. Again without trying to alter your breathing observe how your hands move and whether one moves more than the other.

If you find it hard to feel movement in either position, repeat the exercise concentrating a bit more on your hands. You are breathing so there must be movement somewhere!

Alter the pattern of movement With both hands over the middle of your chest try to increase and then reduce the amount of movement there. Do this with your breathing and not by moving your hands. Similarly vary the movements over your abdomen and the top of your chest with your hands resting on those areas.

When you find you can do that, put your hands in different positions from each other. With one hand over your abdomen and the other at the top of your chest, increase the movement at the abdomen and reduce that at the top of your chest. Then reverse the procedure so that there is more movement at the top of your chest while that at the abdomen is reduced.

This can take a bit of practice but it is a very useful way

to develop control over your breathing so that you can breathe shallowly or deeply at will. When you have reduced the abdominal movement and increased the upper chest movement you are breathing shallowly. When you have increased the abdominal movement and reduced the upper chest movement you are breathing deeply.

When you can do the exercise easily with your hands, do it without using your hands. The aim is to be able to control the level of your breathing, from shallow to deep, and for you to be familiar with the feelings of breathing at these levels. Practise once a day until you can do this easily. Then you have no further need for this exercise.

Remember that you don't need large breaths, just normal breathing. All you are altering is whether your breathing is shallow or deep, and this refers not to the volume of air you take in but to whether it goes to the top or bottom of your lungs.

Calm breathing exercise

This is a very useful and important exercise. Lie on your back. Put a pillow under your head and make sure that you are comfortable. There is no point doing it if you are always thinking how uncomfortable you are.

Put one hand on your abdomen and the other on your chest Breathe through your nose. It is better than through your mouth although if your nose is blocked it is not worth fighting. It is more important to do the exercise.

Let your breath out. Then breathe in gently and deeply. Feel your lower hand rise while the upper hand has much less movement. If you have practised the control exercise above you will be able to breathe deeply rather than shallowly.

Equally gently breathe out again. Take a little longer over the outbreath than you did over the inbreath. As you breathe out you should feel your abdomen fall under your hand. Don't force your breath out; just let it flow naturally as far as it wants to go.

Pause briefly with your lungs empty. Then gently breathe in again and repeat the sequence. It is important that you take longer over the outbreath than the inbreath. This is because it helps you gradually slow the rate at which you breathe.

When you breathe in you are actively using muscles while the outbreath occurs by your muscles relaxing towards their resting positions. If it helps you can use a count such as a clock ticking or a piece of music. This will enable you to measure how long your inbreath takes and thus how long your outbreath should take.

Do this exercise for several minutes several times a day, especially when you feel tense. As you get used to it you will find that you can do it without having to position your hands. You will also find that you can do it sitting or standing so that it becomes a routine you can do unobserved almost anytime anywhere. Use it in the car, at the office, on the production line or in the kitchen and so on.

Since tension and shallow rapid breathing often go together, using a technique like this to slow and deepen your breathing helps enormously to reduce your level of tension.

4
Relaxation

Relaxation is essential to prevent the effects of stress and break the vicious cycle it develops. When you are physically or mentally tense, this increases your level of stress which in turn creates greater tension. Relaxation can help you:

● Cope with the pace of life.

● Manage the pressures of your occupation.

● Improve and promote sleep, especially for those suffering from insomnia.

● Combat fatigue. Stress, and its close colleague worry, make you tense and this can be very tiring. Muscles are not intended to be held permanently contracted. The energy expended on sustaining this state inevitably depletes your reserves and leaves you tired.

● Assist healing. One of the effects of prolonged stress is to decrease your resistance to disease by reducing the efficiency of your immune system. By learning to relax this drag on your innate self-healing capabilities is removed. This helps promote healing and health.

● Improve skilled performance. A lot of occupations and hobbies require very fine and sensitive control of tools and instruments: for example, decorating, needlework, playing a musical instrument or drawing. If your muscles are tense and tight the delicate balance of necessary muscular contractions required to perform the actions will be interfered with.

● Better relationships. You probably know people who are so tense they can be really difficult to get on with. When the tension is prolonged this can have long-lasting effects on relationships, not least being sexual relationships.

● Reduce the frequency and duration of the Fight or Flight reaction. This is when your body prepares to take action in order to deal with an emergency. When we lived in more primitive times these emergencies were usually physical threats and needed a physical response. You either fought or ran away. Now however the threats are not usually physical. They are more likely to be complaints from customers, letters from your bank manager about your overdraft, or bad driving by someone. Physical action is no use. By learning to relax you lengthen your fuse so this reaction is less easily triggered. The Fight or Flight reaction is described in more detail on page 17.

● Increase self-esteem through self-awareness. As you practise relaxation regularly you will become progressively more aware of how tense you used to be and how much has changed. You will feel a lot better about yourself and your self-esteem will rise.

Everyone has the capacity to relax. However modern busy lives often do not leave enough time to space out your activities so that you have sufficient unwinding time between them. Therefore a method of relaxation is needed which will help you relax in a relatively short period. This chapter describes how. It needs to be learnt and practised so that it can be used when needed. You cannot learn to relax only by reading a book or listening to a tape. You must practise as well.

Relaxation is most needed when you are in a high state of tension or anxiety. That is not the time to work out what to do and in what order. Regular daily practice will enable you to master the technique and have it at your finger tips whenever you need it. Also of course, the more you practise, the better you will feel.

Deep Relaxation

To practise relaxation you should set aside time when you will not be disturbed. This is important. If you are at home tell your family not to disturb you. Their co-operation will make it much easier for you to go ahead without worrying what is going on in the house. Arrange with someone to answer the phone if it rings, or else ignore it. You can always unplug the phone if you have a modern system. Do not forget to reconnect it afterwards.

If you are at work tell your colleagues, secretary or boss that you want to be left alone for 20 minutes or so at a convenient time. Although initially it is better to practise relaxation lying down rather than sitting there is no reason, once you are used to it, why you should not sit in your car or at your desk to relax.

Position

Initially practise relaxation lying down. Lie on your back with your hands by your side or resting on your tummy. Make sure that the floor has a soft enough carpet. If necessary, put down a duvet or a couple of blankets. You will probably need a pillow or cushion for your head. If you find lying on your back uncomfortable try putting a pillow under the small of your back. If this is still uncomfortable lie on your side or face downwards. Later on, when you are used to doing it, you can use a chair so that you can get accustomed to relaxing under different circumstances.

Make yourself comfortable. If you are uncomfortable you cannot relax. Take off your shoes and loosen any tight clothing. You need to be warm. If it is winter or there are draughts you might want a blanket over you. However do not get too comfortable since the idea is to achieve relaxation, not go to sleep.

Follow a routine

Relaxation of the whole body is achieved by relaxing different parts of the body in turn. When you have become familiar with the routine you will be able to quicken it up by relaxing larger areas at a time. At first it is best to do it in smaller areas.

The order followed below is only a suggestion. If you prefer to rearrange it there is nothing wrong in that. Nevertheless decide what order suits you best and keep to it. You are not going to be able to relax very easily if you cannot remember what to do next. It may help you to have a friend read the instructions at first. Later on as you become used to them this will not be necessary.

Breathe deeply

Close your eyes. Use the calm breathing exercise described on page 31 for two or three breaths. When your calm breathing is established, on your next breath out allow your whole body to sag and relax. Then direct your attention to the different areas of your body in turn. These areas are described below.

On each breath out let the area you are focussing on relax and sag a little bit more. Don't increase the depth or rate of your breathing or alter it in any way. It should remain calm, even and normal. Just relax the area of your body more with each breath out so that the tension eases as you exhale. Repeat this several times for each area.

Legs

First relax your right leg and then the left. When you are used to relaxing you can do both legs together. Start with your foot.

Wriggle your toes They get tightened up when you are tense. This will help to ease those tight muscles. Often women tend to point their toes down when they are tense and men curl them up.

Roll your ankle around since it is usually held tight too. Your leg will naturally roll outwards when it is relaxed. Check that your ankle is flopped outwards and not pointing straight up.

Relax your foot Use your breathing to help you. As you breathe out let your foot and ankle flop and relax. With each breath let them relax more. Remember not to breathe any deeper than usual. It is as if you are using your breath to carry away the remaining stress and tension in each area.

As you relax your foot and ankle, feel them supported on the floor. The floor is doing all the supporting which needs to be done; there is no need to hold on tight. As you do this a feeling of ease and calm will spread into your foot and ankle.

Your calf Use your breathing in the same way to relax this area and spread the feeling of ease and calm into your calf. Feel the sagging and heaviness as it relaxes and is supported by the floor or bed.

Similarly let the relaxation spread further upwards to the thigh. On each outbreath, let your thigh relax some more.

When you reach the pelvis go back to the ankle and repeat the process, only this time do it more slowly and take longer over each area. If you re-relax each area several times you are not wasting your time or efforts, you are increasing the amount of relaxation there and in your body as a whole.

Relax your other leg when you have finished the first. When you feel confident, relax both legs at the same time.

Relaxation is never wasted however much you do. As you become more practised you will not have to go over the whole of the leg bit by bit. Instead you will be able to relax the leg as a whole by starting at the feet and letting a wave of relaxation spread slowly up to the top. However, until you are used to doing it, it is best to relax area by area.

Trunk

Move to the pelvis, abdomen and trunk. As you breathe out let your pelvis and abdomen relax. Check that you are not clenching your buttocks and that your legs are rolled outwards. This relaxes your hips which are part of the pelvis. Check that you are not holding your abdomen tight. It should feel loose and soft and as you breathe quietly it should rise and fall gently.

Allow your buttocks and back to sink onto the carpet. They should feel heavy and supported by the floor. The floor will take your weight without any help from you so you have no need to hold yourself tight.

Arms

The next area to relax is the arm. First relax your right arm and then your left arm. When you are practised at relaxing you will be able to relax both arms together.

The fingers When you are tense you may clench your hands and fingers. The first thing to do is to stretch your fingers as widely as you can. Then stop stretching and let them flop on to the floor or your abdomen. Without moving your fingers, note what they are touching. Register the sensations such as hard or soft, which come from the tips of the fingers, not by moving them.

Relax your hand Start at your finger tips and progressively work up your arm. As you breathe out let your hand and wrist relax. They should be resting on the floor or chair or your tummy. Feel them supported. Relax your forearm in the same way, and then your elbow and upper arm. Let your arm go so that the floor or chair does the work and not you. You should feel loose and floppy.

Return to your fingers Repeat the sequence but do it more slowly and re-relax each area several times. As you do so the depth of relaxation will increase each time and this will not just be in the one particular area but in the body as a whole.

Relax your other arm when you have finished the first. When you feel confident, relax both arms at the same time.

Head and shoulders

When you are tense you raise your shoulders. As they are held tight they start to ache.

Pull your shoulders towards your feet This stretches the tightened muscles and makes them relax. Pull strongly, not to the extent of hurting, although a little aching is all right. Then stop pulling and let them go.

They may not stay in the position they were in while you were pulling them but that does not matter.

If you have been tense for some time the muscles holding your shoulders will have shortened a little and they will not return to their proper length the first time. This will only happen after regular relaxation. Register that they are further down than before and that your neck feels a bit longer. This helps your brain readjust to the new more relaxed state.

Press your head onto the floor or whatever is supporting it. Then stop pressing and feel it supported. Your head weighs about 10 to 12 pounds and as your brain registers that it is supported the neck muscles will let go.

See if your jaw is tight. Tense people often have their jaws firmly clamped together. Your lips should be gently touching but your teeth should be resting apart from each other. If they are not, keep your lips touching and slightly open your jaws so that the teeth are a little apart. Again register this new more relaxed position.

Return to your shoulders Relax them using your breath as before. Remember not to alter your rate of breathing or how deeply you are breathing. Just breathe normally and as you exhale relax the area.

Move your attention to your neck muscles and then to your jaw, following the same procedure and repeating it several times.

Next move to your eyes and eyelids and lastly your temples. When you relax this area you are also relaxing your mind, so the longer you spend here the more mental relaxation you will achieve.

Having relaxed your whole body, area by area, repeat the procedure if you have time. The more time you spend at it the more relaxed you will become. Concentrate on what you are doing and don't allow yourself to nod off to sleep.

There is much more value in a short but effective relaxation session carried out several times a week than a big one carried out occasionally with you dozing off in the middle of it.

End of session

When you have completed a relaxation session, mentally go through your body and note what all the different relaxed areas feel like. This is very important since it makes your brain notice the more relaxed states. If you do this regularly your brain will start to view the relaxed states as being normal. Then when you become tense your brain will realise that the tense state is not normal and alert you to take action.

It is like resetting a thermostat. You alter the setting to register when action has to be taken. If you adjust your living room thermostat because you are feeling cold then as the temperature falls it will start the heating sooner. Similarly by consciously examining your muscles after relaxation your brain gets used to this lesser degree of tension. It alerts you when this new level of tension is exceeded so that you can take action earlier.

Do not get up suddenly when you have finished your relaxation session. You may feel a little light headed if you do. Instead open your eyes, stretch and yawn a bit and then slowly get up. Allow a few minutes before you start any activities.

5
Exercises

The most frequent result of prolonged tension is aching muscles. The commonest place is the shoulders and trouble here often leads to neck and headaches. Another common place is in the jaw because people often clench their teeth when they are tense. Others experience aches in the bottom of their back. If you look at some of your friends and colleagues you will see the evidence of this tension. Look at their shoulders and jaws when they concentrate or become anxious.

Why do your shoulders or other muscles ache when you are tense? Because your muscles are not built to be held tight all the time. Muscles are intended to contract in order to perform some task and then relax. The way blood is supplied and waste products removed depends on contraction followed by relaxation. If your muscles are held contracted instead of being allowed to relax, waste products accumulate. This is what produces the aching feeling.

Furthermore if a muscle is kept in a contracted state for some time it shortens to adapt to the length it is being held. This is less wasteful of energy than to continually contract it. The result is that the muscle becomes shorter than it was.

Purpose

These exercises have three objectives.
● They stretch your contracted muscles so that they return to their proper length.
● They encourage better blood flow by moving your muscles lightly through a large range of movement.
● They take your muscles from a tense state back towards a proper relaxed state.

Apart from the relief of discomfort this brings, you also become aware of how tense you were. You can then act earlier to deal with tension by using these exercises. This increased awareness behaves like an early warning system enabling you to act before the build up of long term muscular tension develops too far.

Do all the exercises in this chapter slowly and gently. Do not jerk or hurry. If you are in pain do not do an exercise which makes the pain worse.

Hands

People hold their hands very tightly when they are tense. You can see them gripping their fists, twirling their hair, biting their nails or tapping their fingers. Possibly you do too. For a lot of people these actions have become habits, as has the resulting tension in the hand and forearm muscles. When you are tense you close your fist. You do not open your hands in response to tension, you contract them, and the more tense you are the more tightly you grip them.

Compared with other parts of the body your hands have an enormous number of nerve endings which send messages of sensation to the brain. So relaxing your hands sends a much larger number of relaxing messages to the brain than would a similar sized area of your body elsewhere. You can see that it is very helpful to spend time relaxing the hands.

Stretch your hands Open them wide and stretch them as far as you can. Hold the stretch for several seconds and then let go. If your hand is resting on something, the arm of a chair or your thigh or the carpet, let your finger tips fall onto the surface.

Without moving or pressing with your finger tips, sense the surface they are resting on. Is it hot or cold, soft or hard, rough or smooth? Are your fingers separated or together? It does not matter whether they are together or not or what they are resting on. What is important is that you spend time noting these sensations. This sends a flood of messages to your brain which tells it that your hands are at ease and not in a state of tension.

Shake your hands Let your hands and wrists go loose and floppy. Make sure there are no obstacles nearby you might hit. Shake your hands as vigorously as you comfortably can for a minute or so. Then let them rest on your lap or hang loosely by your side. As in the previous exercise, if they are resting on something feel the texture and nature of the surface.

Neck

Turn your head to look over one shoulder See
Drawing 2 below. Turn your head slowly as far as it can go
without hurting. Don't turn your shoulders round: just
turn your head. Don't force your head round or jerk it.
Gently turn it as far as you can. Then without jerking or
snatching, try to turn it a little further. It should not hurt.
If it does you are doing it too hard or you have a problem
which might need the attention of a qualified person. It
should not be a sudden movement but more of a squeeze.
Now turn your head to the other side and repeat. Do this
three to five times.

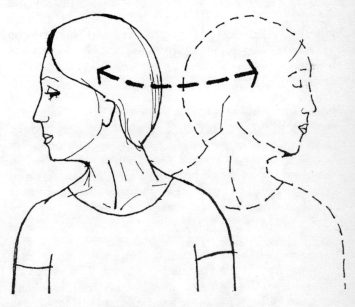

2 Head turn exercise

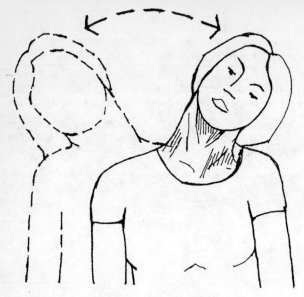

3 Neck bend exercise

Bend your neck to bring your ear down towards your shoulder See Drawing 3 above. It is your ear which should go towards your shoulder and not your shoulder towards your ear. If you lift your shoulder up instead of pulling your head down, nothing is achieved. Do not jerk or snatch your head but bring it smoothly down as far as it can go. Then squeeze it down a little further. You may notice an ache in the other side of your neck when you squeeze but it should not hurt. At the same time as you squeeze your head that extra bit towards one shoulder, pull your arm on the opposite side down. This increases the stretch on the neck and shoulder muscles. Now bend your head to the opposite side and repeat. Do this three to five times.

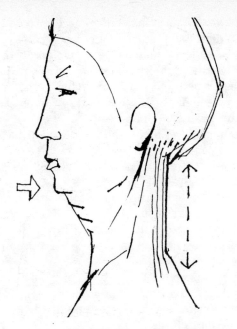

4 Stretch neck exercise

Stretch your neck This stretches the muscles on the back of the neck. Look at Drawing 4 above. Slowly push your head back without leaning backwards or tilting your head, so that if a book were balanced on the top of your head it would not fall off. Tuck your chin in as you move your head back. You may create a slight double chin in the process. As the tight muscles on the back of your neck are being stretched you may feel a pull there. As long as it is not painful that is all right but do not do it too strongly. Hold the position for about ten seconds and then release. Repeat three to five times.

Relax your head This relaxes the muscles which hold up your head. Your head is surprisingly heavy; on average it weighs about 10 to 12 pounds. It is pivoted on the neck behind its centre of gravity and needs muscular effort to keep it level. When you stand or sit with good posture there is only a small amount of muscular activity needed to keep your head up, since its weight is borne by the spine. If your posture is bad the muscles will have a lot more work to do.

Nevertheless, however good your posture, the muscles in the back of your neck are always doing some work except when you are sitting or lying with your head supported. Then they should be at rest. Even then if you are very tense you may still be contracting these muscles. This exercise is to help you relax in that situation so the muscles get a rest.

Lie on your back on the floor with your head on a pillow. Do the calm breathing exercise described on page 31 three or four times so that you are breathing gently and in the lower part of your chest.

Push your head back onto the pillow. Hold the push for only two or three seconds, then let go and feel that the floor is supporting your head. Don't just think it, you have to feel it. Then your brain will tell those muscles to let go and stop wasting valuable energy.

You can also do this exercise sitting in a high backed chair so that your head leans against the back. Push your head against the back of the chair, then let it go so that it is leaning against the chair back and being supported by it. Feel your head being supported by the chair so that your brain issues instructions for those muscles to relax.

Shoulders

Take a large breath and lift your shoulders up. Then drop
them. As you drop them breathe out with a big sigh. You
should empty your lungs completely. Continue to breathe
normally.

Pull your shoulders down The shoulder muscles are
always being contracted and tightened by tension. This
exercise reverses the usual direction of pull.

Pull your shoulders firmly down, away from your ears
and towards your feet. Don't move them backwards or
forwards but straight downwards. Hold them there for
five seconds and then let go. They may ache but they
should not hurt.

You can combine this exercise with the stretch neck
exercise described on page 47 so that you are pulling your
shoulders down at the same time as you are pushing your
head backwards. Practise them separately first to make
sure you have mastered them before you combine them.

Shrug your shoulders This lifts your shoulders up by
shrugging and then drops them. Don't hold them up. Lift
them only so that you can drop them. By doing this you
put the muscles through a cycle of contraction followed by
as complete a relaxation as you can. The normal habit
when tense is to hold them partly elevated. This produces
discomfort. Do not pull your shoulders backwards or
forwards. Let them drop downwards as far as they can go.
Repeat several times.

Roll your shoulders round in as big an arc of movement
as you can. Do it slowly and deliberately one side at a
time. Again the accent is on the stretching phase of the
movement, which is when the shoulder is moving backwards, then downwards and then forwards. Try to make

the movements as big as you can. Repeat the movement several times on each side.

Swing your arms They should be relaxed and floppy and not held tight. If you hold them tight there will be no free movements and the exercise will be a waste of time. Make sure there is plenty of space around you so that your hands do not hit anything.

Lift both hands up in front of you to shoulder level or higher. Then let them fall down past your sides so that they swing back as far as they can under their own momentum, like a pendulum. Repeat the exercise several times. You will find that you get into a rhythm of lift and fall, lift and fall.

A similar exercise is to raise your arms sideways instead of forwards. This time they will swing inwards instead of backwards, and cross in front of you. Again your arms should be relaxed so that they are swinging like pendulums. If your elbows are relaxed you may find that they bend at the end of the swing.

Back and trunk

These exercises help to ease the big muscles in the trunk and low back. Although most people tense up in their shoulders, some also tighten up in their back or tummy muscles. Some people hold their tummies in as if they were braced for a blow there. Others with aches in their low backs feel the pain increases when they are tense. This is not surprising because there is an increase in muscular tension all over your body when you become tense. So an increase in tension in an area where there are already problems is likely to intensify the discomfort there.

First do the calm breathing exercise described on page 31 lying on your back. As you breathe in and out, slowly and gently, your tummy muscles will start to relax.

Relax your back muscles Lying on your back, push your back onto the floor, or whatever you are lying on, and then let go. There is no need to hold yourself. Feel yourself supported by the floor and let go.

Many people remain tight and tense even when lying down. By becoming aware of the support of the floor or whatever you are lying on, you can begin to stop this unnecessary and fatiguing muscle work.

You can also do this exercise sitting in a high backed chair although soft easychairs are not suitable. Press your back into the chair. Then let go and feel yourself supported.

Side bending Stand up and let your arms hang by your side. Now gently bend sideways to one side, sliding one hand down your leg as far as you can go without discomfort or forcing yourself. There are no medals for going further, only aches and pains. Try this several times. Then repeat on the other side. Drawing 5 overleaf illustrates this. If you hear clicks or crunches in your back do not worry unless they hurt. If there is any pain stop the exercise and seek professional advice.

If you have a back problem you may find you can only do this exercise for a very short way before pain starts. In that case stop. Do not hurt yourself.

This exercise is often used quite energetically in keep fit classes. However here it is used to stretch tight trunk muscles and there is no benefit in doing it vigorously. If you find standing for a period of time a problem you can easily do this exercise sitting down. Use a kitchen chair rather than a low easychair, but otherwise it is the same.

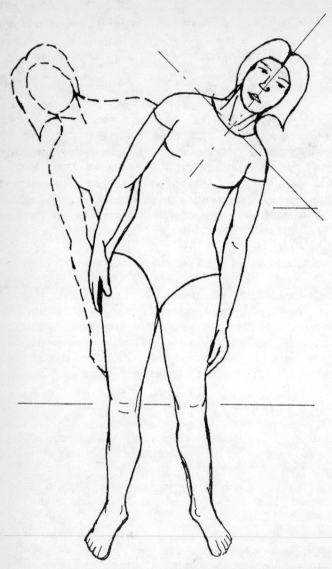

5 Side bend exercise

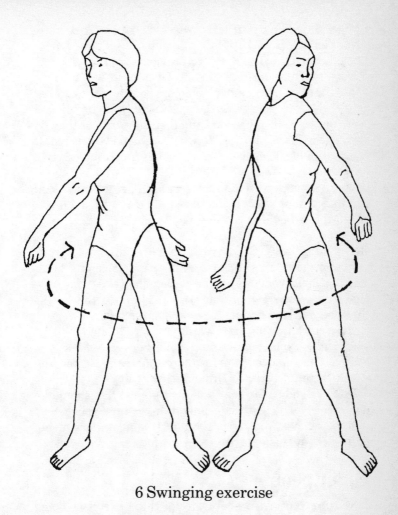

6 Swinging exercise

Swinging This exercise needs space around you. Stand with your feet apart. Let your arms hang loosely by your sides.

Without moving your feet, twist slowly to your right as far as you can go without forcing or hurting. Then twist to the left. See Drawing 6 on the previous page.

Keep twisting to right and left. Go a bit faster, keeping it rhythmical. Remember to keep your arms hanging loosely by your sides. As you get faster your hands will swing away from your sides and float upwards. If they do not you are not letting go. Your arms should be relaxed. If you feel giddy keep your head facing the front or close your eyes.

There is no need to do this exercise energetically. You will find that at a particular speed it feels right and if you go slower or faster it ceases to feel right.

Bend your body Stand with your feet apart and your hands on your hips. Bend to your right. Keeping bent, start to bend your trunk forwards. Then, keeping bent forwards, slowly swing your trunk round to the left so that you end up bending sideways to the left.

Now start leaning backwards and gradually swing to your right while maintaining your backwards lean, so that you have moved your trunk round in a circle keeping it bent throughout. See Drawing 7 opposite.

Do not bend so far that you hurt yourself. It should be done slowly and with concentration so that you get as much stretch as you can without overdoing it and causing pain. Repeat this exercise several times.

Older people

If you are concerned about any of these exercises being bad for you, consult your doctor, osteopath or physiotherapist. Do not do them too vigorously. All are suitable for young and old but of course older people cannot be as energetic as younger folk and you should not expect to be as supple as a younger person. The exercises which

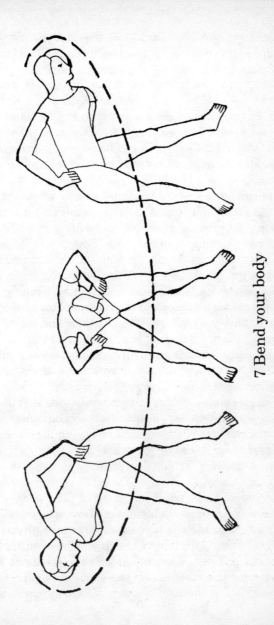

7 Bend your body

involve twisting have to be done more gently and with a smaller range of movement.

Frequency

Stress and tension are recurrent troubles. Therefore these exercises should be used daily, not once a week or once a month. Most of the exercises can be done in a few minutes. To do all of them a few times only takes about ten minutes.

Some are suitable for use in the office or when sitting in your car at traffic lights. Both the office and driving produce a lot of tension so to do something about it there and then is obviously good sense. Some of the exercises have to be done alone in a room and may have to wait until you get home.

Most important is to practise them now. That way you learn them and can recall and do them when needed. It is no use finding yourself in a stressful situation and wishing that you had brought this book with you. Practise now. Practise daily over the next three weeks and not only will you feel the benefit but you will have them at your fingertips for the rest of your life.

If you exercise daily your overall level of physical tension will be reduced. You will also become much more aware of the start of tension. The exercises prevent the effects of tension building up and you will start to see where some of your tension comes from. Some of the causes are obvious but there are other tension-promoting factors which are not so apparent. For instance the telephone ringing, the kids quarrelling or someone honking their horn. As you become more aware of starting to get tense you will notice the irritations which cause trouble. You can then deal with the problems at source and prevent the build up of tension.

6
Self-massage

If you have ever been massaged you will know how pleasant and relaxing it is. You will also know how much it can help with the tensions and aches which occur throughout life. If you have had the bad luck to suffer an injury, massage will probably have been part of your treatment.

Massage is usually given by one person to another. However it is not always convenient to find someone to massage you when it is needed. Sometimes you can massage yourself to ease a particular ache or pain.

Self-massage has the obvious advantage that no-one else is involved but it has a few drawbacks. You can only apply a small amount of pressure to yourself. Since body weight is required to apply pressure it is obviously easier for someone else to apply it, rather than yourself.

You tolerate less pressure when massaging yourself. A person being massaged can relax and let a lot of pressure be applied. Even if it is painful you can accept the discomfort for the benefit gained. The situation is different if you are inflicting pain on yourself. You are much less tolerant of self-inflicted pain than pain inflicted by someone else. If you are massaging yourself it can be awkward to reach some areas and impossible to reach others.

The areas which you can easily reach are described in this chapter. For each area the best position to sit or lie is described but you may have to adapt them to suit yourself. Do not be afraid to experiment if you feel awkward or uncomfortable.

It is impossible to be objective about yourself and your own ailments. This is why you should consult a qualified person and not diagnose yourself. Failure to do this can lead to potentially serious problems being ignored when earlier attention could avert a crisis.

Relax

Since the main purpose of massage is to ease muscles the part of your body should be as relaxed as possible. If you massage muscles which are held partially tense because of the position you are in, you are wasting some of your effort. Get the area as comfortable and supported as possible.

Clothes

Massage is best done on bare flesh. Massaging through clothes is not nearly as effective. If you intend to use oil remove your clothes from the surrounding area as well as from the area to be massaged.

Make sure your hands are clean, whether you decide to massage directly onto your skin or through your clothes. If you massage directly onto skin you could introduce grime and thus infection while if you are doing it through your clothes you would make them dirty.

Order of massage

The massage procedures described start from the neck and shoulders and work down to the feet. There is no need to follow this order. You can massage in any order you like. If you only want to massage your left calf, say, it is pointless going through the other areas first. Nevertheless if you plan to use these techniques regularly it is a good idea to establish your own order and make it a habit. After a little practice you will grasp the methods sufficiently well not to need to refer to this book very often.

Neck and shoulders

The neck and shoulders are best massaged in one of the following four positions. The first is sitting or standing upright. This is probably the most natural one. However, because your neck muscles will be working to support your head you will not be able to relax them completely.

The second is sitting at a table with one elbow resting on the table and your head supported by that hand. This leaves your other hand free to massage.

The third position is sitting in a high backed chair, leaning your head and shoulders against the back. Make sure you are comfortable and there is room either side of the chair for your elbows while you massage. You may need a pillow in the small of your back if the chair back is very straight.

The fourth is lying on your back on the floor. You will need a pillow, preferably a big one, so that your head and neck are lifted off the floor. Lying on a bed is not very satisfactory since the bedclothes get in the way of your hands.

If you adopt one of the last three positions you must let your head and neck go. The purpose of these positions is to encourage the neck muscles to relax as much as possible. Obviously if you are not letting your head, neck and shoulders go the muscles will not relax and the massage is not going to have as much benefit.

Use your right hand to massage your left shoulder, and vice versa. For massaging your neck you can use either hand but you will find it easier if your head is turned away from the side you are massaging. Turn your head to the right when you massage the left side of your neck and shoulders. Look to the left when you massage the right side.

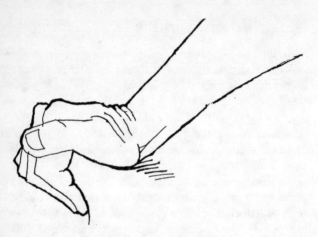

8 Shoulder massage (1)

Massage your left shoulder Put your right hand on your left shoulder. Your hand should lie across your shoulder so that your fingers are on the back of it and the heel of your hand on the front (see page 89). Put a small amount of oil on your hand.

Without moving your fingers slide the heel of your hand towards them. The flesh between the two will get squeezed. As they get closer the heel of your hand will ride up your shoulder until it reaches your fingers. When it has reached your fingers the stroke is completed. Drawing 8 above shows this technique.

Massage the whole of your shoulder Start at the tip, just above the shoulder joint. Gradually work towards the neck and then up the neck to the base of the skull. Each stroke should overlap the previous one by a small amount so as to make sure you do not miss any part of it.

Massage your neck When you get to the neck you may find it more difficult because your hand is too big for the slender muscles there.

   Instead of using the heel of your hand use your thumb. Your index finger, or fingers if you find it easiest to use more than one finger, should remain stationary while your thumb moves towards it. It is easy to pinch so take care not to do that. See Drawing 9 below.

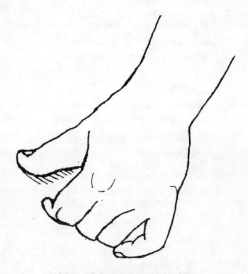

9 Shoulder massage (2)

Go back to the shoulder tip and repeat the massage using a little more pressure. Repeat this several times increasing the pressure each time. When you are applying enough pressure gradually reduce the pressure in the same way as you built it up.

Massage your right shoulder Repeat the above using your left hand.

Base of skull

Run a finger up the back of your neck. When you get to the start of the skull you will feel a slight ridge. It runs to behind each ear. Many of the neck muscles start there. If they are tense the ridge can be quite painful. A lot of neck and headaches can be helped by massage along this ridge.

Put one or two fingers on the ridge so that the pads at the tips of your fingers touch it. Do not use the very tips of your fingers as your nails will dig into you.

Without sliding your fingers over the skin make small circular movements with them. The skin is slightly loose so you can produce a small amount of movement without your fingers moving over the surface of the skin. You do not need any oil since you are not sliding your fingers over the skin. Drawing 10 opposite illustrates the area and position.

If you are not sure about the movement without seeing what you are doing, try massaging the back of your hand. Choose any area and put your index finger on it. Then lightly but firmly move your finger around so that the finger moves and pulls the skin with it. You can make a small amount of movement before your finger slides over the skin. It is this small movement you should apply to the base of the skull.

Follow the ridge at the base of the skull making two

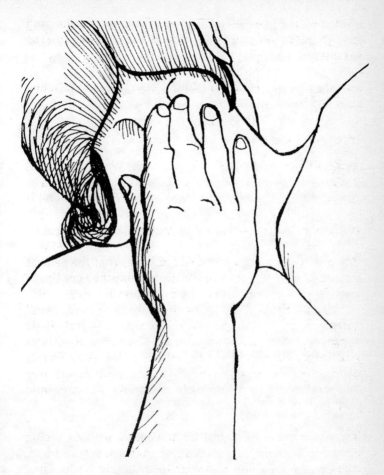

10 Massage the base of skull

or three small circular movements at a time. Then move your fingers on a little keeping light skin contact, and repeat. Use as much pressure as you can comfortably tolerate.

Massage along the length of the ridge to each ear. Start

in the middle and work to your right using the right hand. Then from the middle to your left using your left hand. If you find parts which are tender they are in need of massage. Start lightly over these areas and repeat the massage several times with increasing pressure. Avoid it becoming too painful. The most common sites for these tender spots are either side of the centre of this ridge.

Arms

You can massage your arms fairly easily but you have to find a comfortable position to rest them so that the muscles can relax. There are two convenient positions. The first is sitting with your hand resting on your lap or on a table. The second position is lying on your back with your elbow bent and both your forearm and elbow resting on your tummy. Your upper arm should not touch the floor. If it is you have to stretch awkwardly with your massaging hand to reach it and you will also find massaging the back of your arm difficult.

If you are wearing a tight shirt or blouse you may strain against it. Take it off or replace it with a looser fitting one.

Massaging the arm is described starting from the top of the arm and working downwards, assuming that you are massaging the left arm and that you are sitting with your forearm resting comfortably on your lap.

Upper arm

First massage the outside of your arm. Put a very small amount of oil in the palm of your right hand. Place it over the outside of the left arm just below the knob of the shoulder joint.

Keeping your fingers where they are, move the heel of

your hand towards them until they meet. See Drawing 8 on page 60.

Exert firm pressure onto your arm with the heel of your hand so that the flesh between it and your fingers gets squeezed. When the heel of your hand has reached your fingers you have finished that stroke. Do not be too gentle as you will not do much good, but at the same time avoid being too strong.

If your hands are small you may need to do several strokes to cover the area. Do this as follows. When the heel of your hand has reached your fingers, stretch your fingers further round the arm while keeping the heel of the hand where it is. Then repeat the stroke, bringing the heel of your hand towards the fingers.

Move your hand down your arm keeping light skin contact so that your palm partly overlaps the area you have just massaged and repeat. Continue moving your hand down your arm until you reach the elbow.

Repeat the massage several times with increasing pressure. When you are applying enough pressure gradually reduce to the initial pressure in the same way as you built it up.

Massage the back and front of the arm The method is the same except that your palm should initially be placed on the back or front of the arm. Massaging the inside of the arm is not easy but there is little need for it.

Massage the right side by repeating the above using the left hand.

Forearm

Sit with your left forearm resting on your thigh or on a table so that the palm is facing upwards. Your forearm muscles are divided into two groups. They lie on either side of the arm, running from each side of the elbow towards the wrist. The bulk of the muscles are found in the upper part of the forearm on either side of it so massage is concentrated here.

Put a small amount of oil into the palm of your right hand and place it over the far side of your left forearm just below the knob on the far side of your elbow. Your fingers should be on the back of your arm and the heel of your hand on the front.

Keeping your fingers where they are, move the heel of your hand towards them until they meet. Exert firm pressure with the heel of your hand so that the flesh between it and the fingers gets squeezed. Avoid being too strong. When the heel of the hand has reached the fingers you have finished that stroke.

Move your hand down the forearm keeping light skin contact so that the palm partly overlaps the area you have just massaged and repeat. Continue moving down your arm until you reach the wrist. Drawing 8 on page 60 shows this stroke.

If your hand is too big for the slender muscles in your forearm there is another way. Instead of using the heel of your hand, use your thumb so that the index finger, or fingers if you find it easier to use more than one finger, remains stationary while your thumb moves towards it. It is easy to pinch so be careful to avoid doing that. Drawing 9 on page 61 shows this technique.

Repeat the massage several times with increasing pressure. When you are applying enough pressure gradually reduce to the initial pressure in the same way as you built it up.

Massage the muscles on the near side of the forearm in the same way as above with your hand on the near side of your forearm.

Massage your right arm using your left hand.

Relax your hands

First give your hands a good brisk shake. Then rest one hand on its little finger side, either on a table or on your thigh if you are sitting, or on your abdomen if you are lying on your back.

Hold the index finger just beyond the end knuckle with the index finger and thumb of your other hand. With a firm but gentle pull on the finger, lightly bend it back and forth so that it hinges at the knuckle in its normal way. Then slightly twist it both to the left and to the right. Do not be too strong or enthusiastic; nothing will be gained and you will hurt yourself.

Move your grip so that you are holding just beyond the next knuckle and repeat, and then again with the big knuckle. Do this with all four fingers and thumb. Relax your other hand in the same way.

If you have painful hands or wrists, or arthritis or swollen finger joints consult a doctor, osteopath or physiotherapist before relaxing them. Even then be very slow and gentle and stop if it is painful.

Massage your thighs

Start with the front of your left thigh. Sit upright with your legs stretched out. This relaxes the muscles on the front of your thigh. Put a small amount of oil in the palm of your left hand.

Place your left hand on the front of your left thigh at the

top of your leg. Using the palm of your hand rather than your fingers slide your hand down your thigh until it reaches your knee. (Drawing 15 on page 89 shows the palm of your hand.) This technique is called stroking.

The next stroke should start to the left of the previous one but overlapping it slightly so that no part of the area is missed.

Each subsequent stroke should similarly be slightly to the left of the previous one until you are massaging as far round the thigh as you can reach in this position.

Return to the middle of the thigh and repeat the routine but this time working to the right, towards the inside of the thigh.

Repeat the massage several times, increasing the pressure each time. When you are applying enough pressure gradually reduce to the initial pressure in the same way as you built it up.

To increase the pressure, lean onto your thigh using your body weight and apply pressure that way. Do not push; lean. Apply as much pressure as you want but do not overdo it. Pain is a message that something is wrong and you should not press so hard you hurt yourself.

Massage the front of your right thigh by repeating the above. Use your right hand on the front of your right thigh and massage to the right first and then work inwards.

Massage the outside and back of your left thigh Sit on your right buttock so that you lean over to your right. Your left thigh will be raised off the chair or floor and the outside surface will be partly facing upwards. Drawing 11 opposite shows how to sit.

The method of massage is the same as for massaging the front of the thigh. With a small amount of oil in the

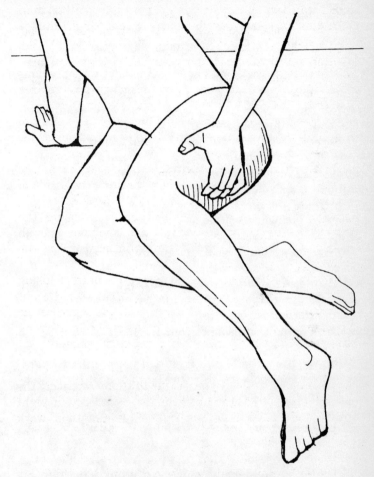

11 Position to massage thigh

palm of your left hand place it on the outside of your left thigh as high up as you can comfortably reach. If you have already massaged the front of your thigh as described above the first stoke should start where you finished the front. If you have not massaged the front of your thigh your first stroke should start at the front of the area you wish to massage. Using your palm slide your hand down the thigh until you reach the knee. The next stroke starts just to the left of the first stroke, overlapping it slightly. Each subsequent stroke should similarly be slightly to the left of the previous one until you reach as far round the back of the thigh as you can.

Repeat the massage several times, increasing the pressure each time. When you are applying enough pressure gradually reduce to the initial pressure in the same way as you built it up.

Increase pressure by leaning onto your thigh using your body weight while you do the stroke. Do not push; lean. Apply as much pressure as you want but do not overdo it. Do not press so hard you are hurting yourself.

Massage the inside of your left thigh Sit on your left buttock and use your right hand. The method is the same as for the outside of the thigh. Use successive strokes moving round the inside of your thigh.

Massage the outside and inside of your right thigh by repeating the above, using your right hand for the outside of the thigh, and your left hand for the inside of the thigh.

Both hands You can use both hands together to massage the front, inside and outside of the thigh. They should start off side by side so that they touch in the middle of the thigh. Both hands should move at the same time.

When you have finished a stroke the next one should start with the hands a little further apart. Each hand should slightly overlap the area covered by the previous stroke so that nothing is missed. Successive strokes should be further apart until your hands cannot reach any further. If necessary, repeat with greater pressure.

Massaging the back of the thigh with both hands is not practical.

Kneading your thighs

Having finished the stroking technique you should knead the area.

Knead the front of your left thigh Sit with your legs stretched out. With a small amount of oil in your right hand put your palm on the middle of the front of your thigh at the top of the leg. Your fingers should point towards the outside of your leg.

Keep your fingers where they are and move the heel of your hand towards them so that you squeeze the flesh between the heel of your hand and fingers. Drawing 8 on page 60 shows the technique.

An alternative method is to knead between your thumb and forefingers. Your posture and hand position are the same as before, but instead of moving the heel of your hand towards your fingers move your thumb towards your fingers. The flesh should be squeezed between your thumb and fingers. Drawing 9 on page 61 shows the technique.

Knead round the thigh Do several strokes, each following on from the previous one. At the end of a stroke the heel of your hand, or thumb if you are using that method, should remain where it is. Stretch your fingers out so that they rest further round the thigh. Then knead towards your fingers with the heel or thumb of your hand as before. Repeat this until you have reached as far round the thigh as you can. Return to where you started keeping light skin contact.

The next stroke starts back at the middle of the thigh, but half a handwidth lower down the leg so that you are overlapping the previously kneaded area. With successive strokes overlapping, work from the top of your thigh down to your knee.

When you reach your knee return to the top of the thigh.

Repeat the massage several times, increasing the pressure each time. When you are applying enough pressure gradually reduce to the initial pressure in the same way as you built it up.

Next use your left hand. Place it on the front of your thigh, in the middle at the top of the leg. Your fingers should point towards the inside of your thigh. Using the same method as you did with your right hand knead the front of your thigh working towards the inside of the thigh. Massage from the top of the leg down to the knee, repeating with greater and then lesser pressure.

Knead further round the outside of your thigh Sit on your right buttock so that you lean over to your right. Your left thigh will be raised off the chair or floor and the outside surface will be partly facing upwards. See Drawing 11 on page 69.

The method of kneading is exactly the same as for kneading the front of the thigh. If you have already kneaded the front of your thigh the first stroke should start where you finished. If you have not kneaded the front of your thigh your first stroke should start at the front of the area you wish to massage.

Knead the inside of your left thigh Sit on your left buttock so that you are leaning over to your left and use your right hand. The method is the same as for kneading the outside of the thigh.

Knead your right thigh Repeat the above but replace your left hand by your right and your right hand by your left.

Lower leg

The calf muscles are on the back of your lower leg and form the bulge below the knee.

There are two positions to reach them. The first is sitting on a stool or chair with your knees bent and your feet on the floor. Your feet should be in front of you. Do not straighten out your legs. This elongates the calf muscles tightening them up. It also means you have to stretch to reach the area and this can make massaging difficult.

The second position is sitting with one leg crossed over the other so that the ankle of one leg rests on top of the knee of your other leg. See Drawing 12 overleaf. You can then easily reach the calf with either hand though it is easier to use the opposite hand. Thus if you massage your left calf you would have your left leg crossed over your right so that the left ankle is resting on your right knee. Then you would use your right hand to massage it.

Kneading the calf Place your hand with a little oil on it over your calf so that the palm lies over the belly of the muscle. Keeping your fingers where they are, move the heel of your hand towards them so that the muscle gets squeezed. Drawing 8 on page 60 shows the method.

You may find it easier to use your thumb rather than the heel of your hand. To do this move your thumb towards your fingers so that the muscle gets squeezed between it and the fingers.

Work from the top of the calf under the knee downwards, with each stroke overlapping the previous one so that you do not miss any part.

If your hands are small and you have relatively large calves you may have to do two or three strokes working across the calf before moving further down it in order to cover the whole of the muscle. At the end of a stroke the

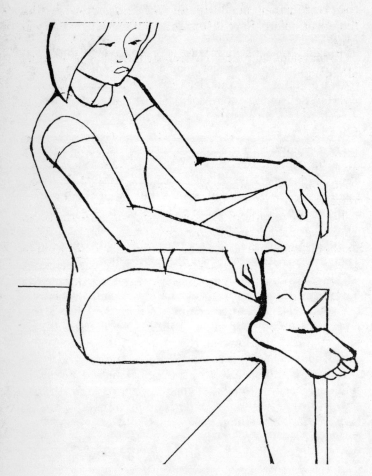

12 Position to massage calf

heel of your hand, or thumb if you are using that method, should remain where it is. Stretch the fingers out so that they rest further round the calf. Then knead towards the fingers as before. Repeat this until you reach as far as you can go.

To massage your other calf repeat the above using your other hand.

Feet and ankles

Your feet and ankles may ache quite a lot from the misuse they get. Modern life requires fashion shoes and hard, even surfaces to walk on. Feet are better suited to no shoes and soft undulating surfaces. Massage can help refresh tired feet.

If you have painful toe joints, swelling or arthritis in your toes, check with your doctor, osteopath or physiotherapist before starting to massage them. Even then be very slow and gentle and stop if it is painful. Otherwise as long as you do not hurt yourself, your movements can be fairly strong.

Relax your toes To work on your left foot, remove your left shoe and sock and sit on a chair. Cross your left leg over your right so that your left ankle rests on the top of your right knee. With your right hand, hold the toes as a group while your left hand holds the foot below the ball of the foot. Now holding your foot still with your left hand move the toes up and down and then round with your right hand. See Drawing 13 below.

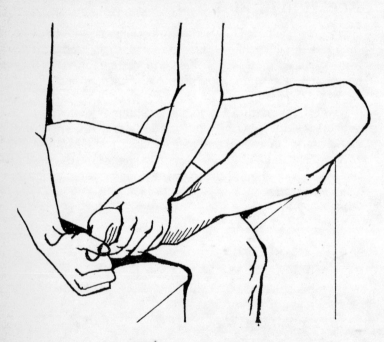

13 Relaxing your toes

Relax your ankles With your leg in the same position, hold your left ankle with your left hand and with your right hand hold your foot over the ball of the foot. Use your right hand to move the foot around in a circular fashion while holding it still at the ankle with your left hand. Then, keeping the hand position unchanged, move the foot with your right hand backwards and forwards. See Drawing 14 below.

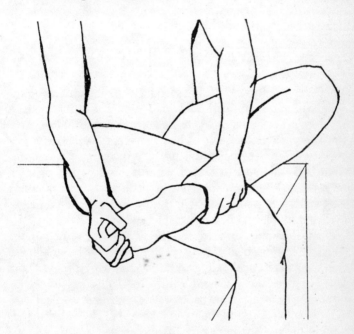

14 Relaxing your ankle

Relax both feet Do the same movements on your other (right) foot but reverse your foot position and hand holds.

7
Massage

Massage is not new. People have been giving and receiving massage for thousands of years. But it is a skill and like other skills needs to be learnt. This book teaches you the various techniques but there is no substitute for practice. Read the text and use the drawings to explain what to do and how to do it. Then put the instructions into action. At first you may feel a little awkward or self-conscious. That is natural but it will soon pass and be replaced by pleasure and satisfaction.

A lot of people say they are the wrong sort of person to learn massage because they do not have a medical, nursing or technical background. Do not worry about this. The people I have taught come from all sorts of backgrounds, varying from doctors to canteen staff, from skilled workers to unemployed labourers. They all started having previously done very little massage (if any) and at the end have been able to massage confidently and competently. You can do it as well.

Massage is usually associated with relief from pain or discomfort. Another reason for learning massage is concerned with pleasure. Having someone touch and caress you can be very enjoyable and that pleasure can be enhanced by using massage. Massage skills enable you to give greater pleasure and while this book does not deal with the sexual aspect of touch there is no reason why massage should not be used with great success in the sexual field.

How to start

This chapter gives general advice on how to give a good massage. The following chapters tell you how to massage specific parts of the body. Each chapter is self contained. This enables you to pick a chapter which is needed and use it without referring to other chapters. For instance you might only want to massage the lower back or neck. However it means that if you read the book right through there is a certain amount of repetition.

A small amount of descriptive anatomy, where the muscles and bones lie, is given so you have some idea of the structure of the body. Although you can give a good massage relying on your intuition, a knowledge of what lies under your hands makes the massage much more effective.

The person receiving the massage should be relaxed, warm and comfortable. If tense or embarrassed it will take time and effort to calm and relax him or her before getting down to the massage.

One word of warning: this book does not teach you about diagnosis or medical treatment. Before you massage ask yourself if you know why the area hurts and whether a doctor, osteopath or physiotherapist should check it first.

Often the problem is small with an obvious cause, for example if you have just finished a long car drive and have aching shoulders. However there are some aches which are not so easily explained. The danger with massaging them in the hope they will go away is that proper diagnosis and treatment are delayed at the cost of the person's health and well being. Common sense is the guideline. If in doubt do not massage. Ask first.

Where to massage

The room where you massage is important as it helps establish the atmosphere. You want an environment which is relaxing and friendly without being too intimate. The person you massage is letting you get very close and the surroundings should reflect that. If the atmosphere is wrong it is much harder for the person to relax and that will reduce the effect of your massage.

Privacy is very important. People cannot relax if they are embarrassed. Massage is a private affair because it involves letting someone else look at and touch your body. If there are other people looking on, or if there is a possibility that others could look, the person being massaged will feel ill at ease. Don't massage in the hallway or kitchen where friends and family pass through.

On the other hand, do not use intimate rooms like bedrooms for massaging people you do not know well, particularly if they are of the opposite sex.

The room should be reasonably tidy. You do not want to fall over toys or other obstacles. If the room is untidy you may feel embarrassed which will interfere with your massage. However the room should not be too clinical. If you are in your own home the person you are massaging may anticipate a homely feel, and a room which is too clinical can be offputting.

Warmth

To massage effectively you must use your bare hands on the person's bare skin. Since you are likely to use oil not only should the area you massage be unclothed but some of the surrounding area too. You will feel very cramped if only a small area is exposed, and you may dirty the person's clothes with oil.

The room must be kept warm: about 70°F The body loses a lot of heat when unclothed. Unless your massage is confined to a very small area the person being massaged will have to remove a lot of clothing. He or she will be lying still while you do the massage. You may feel warm and if you are massaging vigorously you may get quite hot. However the person receiving your massage must be kept warm too.

Draughts are another problem. If there is an open window or the door is not closed properly or has a gap at the bottom, there may be a draught and the person being massaged will be much more aware of this than you.

Towels

Some people feel the cold more easily than others so have some large towels handy. If the person is cold you can cover the areas not being massaged.

The person you are massaging may find being un-clothed embarrassing. Even when someone has asked for massage they may not like exposing their body to you. You should not feel surprised or offended. Use towels to cover the areas not being massaged at that moment. Then when you move to another area reposition the towels to minimise the exposed area.

Atmosphere

Be reasonably sure you will not be interrupted. It is disruptive for you as well as annoying for the person being massaged if you keep on having to stop and then start again. If possible get someone to look after children if they are small or tell them what is happening and not to interrupt you if they are older.

Telephone calls cannot be predicted. Unplug the phone if you can. Alternatively get someone else in the house to handle calls.

The lighting in the room contributes to the atmosphere you create. Fluorescent lights make for a hard cold clinical atmosphere while dim concealed lights create warm intimate surroundings.

Some people like background music, others do not. If you or the person you are massaging want background music, consider whether your tastes are compatible. If you like pop music and he or she prefers Mozart it would be better if you did without.

Finally remember that although you are massaging someone for their aches, pains or stress, the experience should be as pleasurable as possible.

What to lie on

What should the person being massaged lie or sit on. There are five alternatives: a table, a chair or stool, the floor, a bed or a proper massage table. I recommend a table for most massage but you may prefer the other options.

A table

A table is usually the best solution. Obviously if you are only interested in massaging someone's forearm then to go to the trouble of positioning the table and possibly rearranging the rest of the lounge furniture is a waste of time and effort. However it is different if you massage a larger area such as the back. In this case having a surface on which the person receiving the massage can lie comfortably, while you have good access to their back with plenty of room to move, is very important. Indeed it is essential if your massage is to be effective without being awkward for you.

The table should be strong, stable and long enough. It has to be accessible on one side although it is better if you can walk all the way round. The table must be strong. You do not want the person you massage crashing to the ground amidst a collection of splinters, any more than you want some valuable piece of furniture destroyed by being lain on by a large friend.

It is equally important that the table should be stable. If you are lying on a wobbly table one thing that you are not going to do is relax. In fact you will tense up and thus undo any benefit from the massage.

The length of the table might pose a bit of a problem since not every one has a traditional dining table. The parts of the body which need continuous support are the head, trunk and thighs. However, the calves, ankles and feet can be supported just at the ankle. Use the back of a settee or chair, padded with cushions, to support the ankles. The height of the table and the posture of the person doing the massage are very important. They are discussed in more detail later in this chapter.

A chair

A chair or stool is very useful if your massage is confined to the neck and shoulder area. Many people have a lot of aches in that area. The trouble with using a chair is that it makes massaging the rest of the body difficult. With a bit of thought you can do some fairly effective massage on the lower and upper back and this is very useful if you are trying to help someone who is elderly, or who for some reason cannot be moved easily onto a table or the floor. An advantage of some chairs is that they are ajustable and this makes the problem of getting your posture right a lot easier. You can also massage some parts of the legs.

The floor

The most obvious choice is to use the floor. You have to make sure the carpet is clean or covered with a clean sheet or towel and you should avoid hidden draughts.

There are two problems with using the floor: the posture you adopt when giving the massage, and the fact that you have to keep getting up and moving to work on a different area.

Giving someone an overall massage on the floor can be an awkward and disjointed procedure. It often leaves you with an aching back. Posture and how to avoid hurting yourself while giving massage is discussed on page 90.

If you only have to massage one small area, for example the shoulders or the calf, you will not need to move around very much and some of the objections to using the floor disappear. Nevertheless the problems it creates for your posture remain.

A bed

Beds have two main disadvantages. They are generally too low for massage and they are almost always too soft. The surface needs to be comfortable but very firm. You are going to apply quite a bit of pressure from time to time, and if all that effort goes into stretching bed springs you will expend a lot of effort with no end result. Some beds are very firm and if you have one of these it might be adequate, although you still have to deal with the problem of your posture.

Professional massage table

Professional masseurs use specially designed treatment

tables called plinths. They are expensive and take up a lot
of space. The electrically operated adjustable professional
plinths retail for several hundreds of pounds at the
cheapest and go over a thousand for the more sophisti-
cated models. You can buy portable plinths which fold up
like pasting tables but even these retail for something like
£150 and would not be worth considering unless you plan
to take up massage in a serious way. If you or a friend are
handy at making things and could construct one, this of
course becomes a worthwhile solution. If you intend to do
this, read the section on posture on page 90 first to ensure
it is the right height.

Comfort

Whatever the person is lying on must be comfortable. The
surface should be soft but firm. Several blankets or a
duvet on a hard surface will help. Some people find their
ankles are uncomfortable when they are lying face
downwards. This is often because they point their toes. If
so put a small pillow under the ankle.

Oil

There is an impression that oil is of great importance in
massage and without the correct oil it will not be a
success. In fact the role of oil is a much more humble one.
It is used as a lubricant, just as it is in your car. You need
some sort of lubricant to reduce the friction between your
hands and the skin of the person you are massaging. If
you rub your hands together they get warm because of the
friction produced. You do this in winter for precisely that
reason. This is fine when it is cold but is not usually
required when massaging someone.

A good oil to use is sweet almond oil, often available
from health food shops. A widely available oil is baby oil,

which is cheap and easily purchased at chemists. Even oils like salad or cooking oil are alright although draw the line at oil that has been used for frying!

Use a small amount of oil at a time. Put it into the palm and fingers of your massaging hand. When it is used up and you feel some friction, put a little more into your hand. You need oil whenever you are sliding or moving over the skin.

Health food stores often sell a selection of massage oils. Some have additives which give a pleasant smell and are meant to help various problems. Take these claims with a pinch of salt, but even if they do all that is claimed they are rather expensive when what you are after is basically a lubricant.

Oil is absorbed through the skin in very small amounts. Only when you do a lot of massage should you concern yourself with the quality of the oil. If you are going to massage occasionally you need not worry. The exceptions are if you are massaging infants or very sick people. Their skin will absorb the oil and poor quality oils could impose another burden on them.

Talcum powder

Another option is to use talcum powder although it does have some disadvantages. Firstly it spreads a lot further than the area to be massaged, and if you use too much it goes everywhere whereas with oil you can easily wipe up any excess. Secondly if you massage someone who is perspiring a lot the talc tends to coagulate with the sweat, losing its effectiveness as a lubricant as well as being somewhat unpleasant. Lastly you may not like the perfume which is added to talc. On the plus side it is readily available in chemist shops and you may like the perfume and handling it. Also if you accidentally knock it over it does not run all over the place, and is easier to clean up than oil.

Cream

The last option is to use one of the rubbing creams you can buy from chemists, such as Deep Heat. Do not use these at first. They can be very useful for particular problems but they are not a good idea for the beginner to use for general purpose massage. They may also sting if you get them on delicate skin like the mouth or lips and especially the eyes.

Jewellery

Jewellery should not be worn if it is in the area you massage. It is very difficult to massage around necklaces or bracelets and after you have finished the massage there will be traces of oil left on the jewellery. Ask the person to remove any jewellery and if you are going to massage the neck make sure that earrings are removed. If they have studs they can scratch you and if they are large you may inadvertantly catch them and hurt the person's ear.

If you are wearing rings, remove them. They can dig into the skin and hurt. If you are wearing a smooth ring this may not hurt but ask the person while you are massaging if it does rather than assume that it does not. Certainly if your ring has stones in it make sure that they are not on the palm side of your hand if you do not want to or cannot remove it.

Take off your watch. Metal watch straps can scratch if they rub on the skin. The watch can also get in your way when your hand tilts back while you massage. Bracelets should also be removed. They do not usually scratch but they may rub the skin. This can tickle or irritate the person being massaged who is unlikly to relax. They will also collect oil and debris from the skin and need washing after your massage.

The masseur

You need to be at ease when massaging. If you are uncomfortable or tense the flow of your massage will be disturbed. This often results in tentative jerky movements rather than easy flowing strokes. One of the causes is uncertainty of what to do, when to do it, and how much pressure to use. Reading this book and practising the various techniques will help you sort this out. However there are other factors which contribute to this problem:

Clothing

Wear loose, comfortable clothes. A tracksuit would be suitable. Avoid tight fitting clothes. You will stretch and twist quite a lot and your clothes should not restrict you. You must be able to move around freely. If you are massaging a small person you will not use a lot of energy. However if the person is large you may become quite energetic. In this case you can get very warm. Do not open the windows because the person you are massaging will get cold and start to shiver and tighten up. Rather choose clothes which will keep you cool or wear a jersey or cardigan which can be removed when you are warm and put back on when you have finished.

Do not massage wearing high heels or tight shoes. Use low heeled comfortable shoes, trainers, or take your shoes off and go barefoot. If your feet are uncomfortable or restricted you will not relax. If you are wearing high heels you will not be stable enough to exert the amount of pressure necessary for massage. Massage is a physical activity and you need to be comfortable to do it effectively.

Hands

Your hands should be clean. Dirty hands will not inspire confidence in the mind of the person being massaged. Also important is the length of your nails. In the stroking movements of massage you mainly use the palm of your

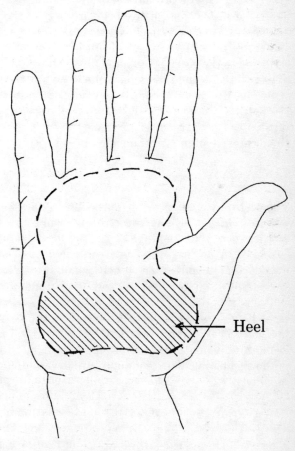

15 Palm and heel of hand

hand while in the kneading movements your fingers are used more. If you plan to massage a lot you will have to accept that your nails must be short. Check with the person you are massaging if your nails are digging in or scratching. They should not be.

Heel and palm of the hand Most of the massage strokes described in the rest of the book use either the palm of your hand or just the heel of your palm. The palm covers the entire area of your hand from where the fingers join the hand to the start of the hand above the wrist. The heel of your hand is the area where the hand starts above the wrist. It runs from the start of your thumb to the other side of the hand. Drawing 15 on the previous page illustrates these areas. The palm is the entire area within the dashes. The heel is the shaded area.

Posture

The posture you adopt while massaging is very important. If you hold yourself incorrectly you will tire easily, be inefficient in your massage and, even worse, risk injuring yourself. In massage you use your own body weight to exert pressure on the person being massaged. You lean on the person. You do not push with your arms.

The part of the body you wish to massage must be at the right height for you to be able to lean. If the height is too low you will stoop and eventually your back will hurt. If it is too high you will be unable to apply enough pressure without pushing with your arms and you will tire very quickly.

The right height

There is a simple rule of thumb to get the correct height. Stand next to the surface on which the person you are going to massage will lie. With your arm by your side your finger tips should rest comfortably on the surface. See Drawing 16 overleaf. However body sizes vary quite considerably. If you massage a skinny person the height you have just tested may be a little too low. If the person has the dimensions of a heavyweight wrestler it may be too high.

Adjust the height

If you use a dining or kitchen table it may be the wrong height. If it is too high stand on something in order to get yourself to the correct height. It does not matter what you choose to stand on as long as it is stable. Telephone directories or large books are useful.

If the table is too low do not stoop: this is bad for your back. Put something under the legs of the table to raise it to the correct height. Failing that stand with your legs astride and knees bent a little so that your trunk is lower. This may seem a little strange at first because the natural inclination is to bend over in a stoop. Practise it a few times. You will soon get used to it although your legs may get tired at first.

Try massaging at different heights. Do not be afraid to experiment. Make yourself too high as well as too low. You need to feel you are at the right height and to know the difference between that and being too high or too low. Once you have worked out the correct height it is easy to find it again.

Lean – use your body weight

To massage effectively you must use your own body weight to lean on the person you are massaging. Do not push with your arms.

Practise leaning. Stand facing the table or surface on

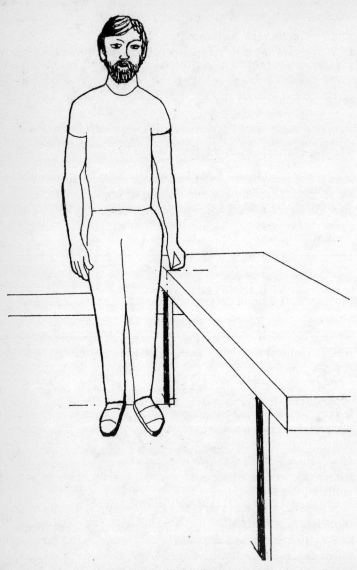

16 The right height

which you propose to massage. Put both hands in front of you onto the surface. Lean on it. Keep your back straight and your elbows slightly bent so that your body weight is behind your hands. Avoid stooping. You should be comfortably leaning without any strain or effort and should be able to carry on a conversation for quite a time.

When you need to increase the amount of pressure you apply to a particular area, do so by transferring more of your body weight to your hands and reducing the amount on your feet. Never take both feet off the ground with all your weight on your hands. You will not be stable and cannot control the massage. At times you may have to go up on your toes if you need to apply a lot of pressure. This often happens when a small, light person is massaging a well built heavy person.

Get close

Now that you have the right height and correct posture, the next thing is to make sure that you are near enough. Return to the table or surface you are using and place a pillow or cushion in the middle of it. Stand next to the surface facing it. Work on the pillow as if you were kneading a lump of dough. Do not forget to lean rather than push.

Now move the pillow further away from you and work on it again. Then move it right next to you. You will notice that it is a lot easier when it is closer to you. You may find that your low back starts to ache when the pillow is on the other side of the surface. It will ache even more if you continue for longer.

Still using the pillow or cushion try varying the amount of pressure you are exerting. Do this with the pillow close to you, then with it in the middle and lastly on the far side of the table. You will find it much easier to apply pressure when the pillow is closer to you. Your low back is vulnerable when you stretch and in any case stretching is an inefficient way of applying pressure.

Practise

There is no substitute for actually doing something in order to learn it. If you have someone to practise on so much the better but if not practise with a pillow. Once you have the feel of it you will be confident when the need or opportunity arises to use it in earnest. Practise varying the height, closeness and amount of leaning and pressure so that you feel comfortable.

The people you massage may not be aware that you are at the wrong height or wrongly positioned but your back will be and so will your aching muscles. With a little practice you will be able to massage for a substantial time without tiring yourself.

Do not push

Pushing leads to problems:
● You get tired very quickly. If you only massage a small area, say the calf, you may not notice it. However if you want to massage someone's back, particularly if the person is large and well muscled, you will soon tire. Professional masseurs can massage several people one after the other with only a very short break. If they were pushing and therefore using a lot of muscles and energy they would not be able to manage this. Of course you will use some muscles more than you have done before so they will feel a bit tired initially. This is inevitable with any new physical activity. By using your body weight you will save a lot of energy and the process will be much more enjoyable.
● The muscular effort of pushing leads to unevenness in your massage. A smooth even flow is essential for a good

massage. If your arms are held rigid, which often happens when you are pushing, this evenness of flow will be disturbed. The actual effort of pushing only makes the situation worse.

● The sensitive touch a good masseur develops is inhibited by pushing. When you are massaging someone there is a two way flow of sensations taking place. The person receiving the massage is feeling what you are doing but at the same time you are feeling the tissues which you are touching. With practice you will be able to appreciate the different feel of tight muscles, of healthy and unhealthy skin and so on. This needs sensitivity on your part and anything that interferes with or reduces your sensitivity is undesirable. Tension does this and so does concentration on making a muscular effort. Pushing when you should be leaning produces both tension as well as muscular effort.

● You risk injuring yourself by pushing. If you overuse a muscle or group of muscles they are at risk of being strained. Any physical activity can cause injury if the muscles involved have not been sufficiently trained for that level of activity. This is true whether you are involved in a sporting activity or doing something like restarting gardening after the winter break. It may seem unlikely that massage has the same risk and done properly it is highly unlikely that it will. Bad technique in any activity can lead to problems. In massage, if you can use your body weight correctly you will also have a good posture and this will reduce the risk of straining your back.

Summary

● Atmosphere, warmth, privacy and comfort are important.

● Oil or talc is used as a lubricant.

● A table is the best surface for the person you massage to lie on.

● The person should lie at the right height. If the surface is too low, raise it or work with your legs astride. If it is too high stand on something stable to raise yourself to the right height.

● Use your body weight to apply pressure. Lean. Do not push.

● Make sure that the person you are massaging is close to you. You should be standing right beside the table and the person you massage should be as near you as possible without feeling as though he or she is likely to fall off.

● Practise until you get the feel of it.

8
Low back massage

Hundreds of thousands of people suffer with pain in the lower part of their back and millions of working days are lost every year as a result. The symptoms range from an occasional mild ache to sheer agony, from discomfort in a small area at the bottom of the back to shooting pains and numbness from the waist to the tips of the toes.

Low back ache can have many causes and it is essential before you attempt any massage that you have a proper diagnosis, either from a doctor, qualified osteopath or physiotherapist. The symptoms may be helped by massage but equally they may not. It needs professional skill and training to tell the difference.

Many terms are used to describe back ache. Unfortunately they are often misused by doctors and other professional people who should know better:

Lumbago means an ache in the lower part of the back and is no better than the expression backache. It mostly describes a dull nagging or gnawing ache, usually in the area just above the buttocks. Often the trouble is tight muscles due to over exertion, for example too much digging or housework, and is frequently combined with some normal wear and tear in the spinal joints.

Slipped discs sound more dramatic and frequently the symptoms leading to that diagnosis are. They are often very painful. However discs do not slip. The discs are pads of gristle which lie between adjacent bones in the spine. They act as shock absorbers as well as allowing the individual bones of the spine to move without grinding each other to pieces. They are very firmly attached to the bones on either side of them and do not move from their positions. However they can degenerate although it is not fully understood why. This leads to the discs becoming thinner which can cause many of the symptoms of back ache.

Trapped nerves conjure up the image of nerves being squeezed or squashed between the bones of the spine. While in very serious cases involving fractures of the spine this may happen, the term is usually more imaginative than accurate. The symptoms of trapped nerves are often the same as for slipped discs, and similar sets of symptoms often receive either diagnosis.

Sciatica has a more precise meaning but is often loosely used. It usually refers to discomfort which spreads down the leg. In fact it means pain or other symptoms running along the course of the sciatic nerve. This nerve is the largest in the body and runs from the bottom of the back down the back of the leg all the way to the toes. If the nerve is affected by something and pain is felt along the course of the nerve then the term sciatica is used. However, it is a label and not a diagnosis. It does not describe what has happened to the sciatic nerve or why it is producing those symptoms. It only says that the symptoms come from the sciatic nerve.

The lower back

This chapter describes massaging the back from the buttocks to below the shoulder blades. Chapter 9 deals with the upper part of the back and takes you from the shoulder blades to the base of the neck. If you want to massage the whole of the back read about and practise on each area separately at first and then put them together. As you grow confident you can massage the whole back without having to divide it into smaller sections.

To start off you should deal with each area as a separate unit. Look at Drawing 17 overleaf. You can see that one part shows the area as you see it while the other shows some of the muscles which lie under the skin. Try to get a mental picture of what lies beneath the skin. This will make your massaging much more effective and interesting. To help you familiarise yourself with the area, start off with a simple exercise.

Correct position

The person to be massaged should lie on his or her front. The arms should be either by the side or over the edge of the table. The back should be unclothed from the buttocks upwards.

If massaging a man ask him to take off his shirt and vest. Also get him to loosen his belt and push his trousers down so that the tops of the buttocks are free. If you are massaging a woman ask her to do the same, loosening her skirt and taking off a full length slip. When she is lying down undo her bra, though if it undoes at the front she will have to undo it just before she lies down.

There is no point in trying to massage through clothes. It will not be effective and is a waste of time. If you only uncover a very small area you will find yourself very restricted and will probably get oil on the person's clothes.

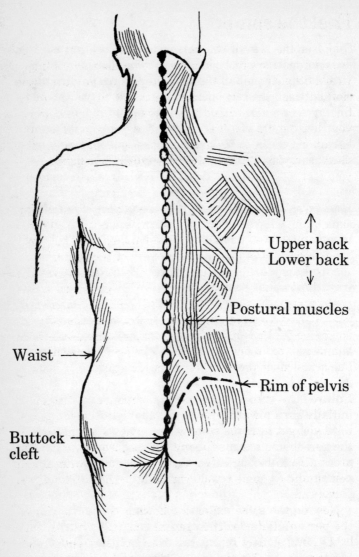

Upper back
Lower back

Postural muscles

Waist

Rim of pelvis

Buttock cleft

17 The back

Feel the spine

Stand at the side of the person next to the buttocks. It does not matter which side you are standing. Put a finger with a little oil on it on the back just above the start of the cleft between the two buttocks. It is best to use the index finger of your right hand if you are right handed, and of your left hand if you are left handed. You should feel the hard bone of the spine under your finger. If you do not, move your finger round the area lightly but firmly until you do.

Run your finger up the spine, slowly and gently feeling each knob of the spine. Note that there is a knob followed by a gap followed by another knob and so on. The knobs are the tips of the bones or vertebrae of the spine.

Next run your finger back down the spine towards the start position but stop about three inches above the buttock cleft. Move your finger off the spine and towards you. At first the area under your finger becomes softer as you move off the bone. Then you will find that it goes hard again as you touch more bone before you reach the buttock. This is part of the rim of the pelvis.

Follow the rim of the pelvis with your finger It initially runs towards the head and slightly towards you until you get near the waist when it turns downwards. If the person you are massaging is fleshy you may have to press a little harder. This exercise is easier with a thin person and on some people you can see the outline of the pelvic rim.

Now do the same exercise following the pelvic rim on the person's far side. Then repeat the exercise with your other hand. Lastly repeat the exercise using both hands together, only this time each hand will follow different sides of the pelvic rim.

Postural muscles

Look at the back carefully. On each side of the spine the surface bulges a bit. Further away from the spine towards the side the bulge disappears. Look further up the back. Notice that the bulge runs up each side of the spine. This bulge is made up of the postural muscles. These muscles maintain your posture and are very often affected by back ache. Trace the bulge with your fingers. You should familiarise yourself with it since it is important in back massage.

Now look at Drawing 17 on page 100 again. Try to match it with what you have felt. The better your sense of touch and the more accurate grasp you have of the anatomy or layout of the area, the better your massage will be.

Stroking the lower back

Stand at the person's side, level with the hips. It does not matter which side. Stand so that you are half turned away, facing towards the head. Your feet should be apart with your outside foot pointing towards the head. See Drawing 18 opposite.

Put a small amount of oil onto your hands Avoid using too much. When this has been absorbed take some more. Place both hands so that the whole of your palms lie on the back where the buttocks merge into the bottom of the spine. See Drawing 19 overleaf. Your hands should rest either side of the spine with your fingers pointing towards the shoulders. Your thumbs, which don't do any work with this stroke, should be virtually touching each other. They should be over the spine and just resting on the skin without applying pressure. Don't massage the spine itself, there is no muscle there.

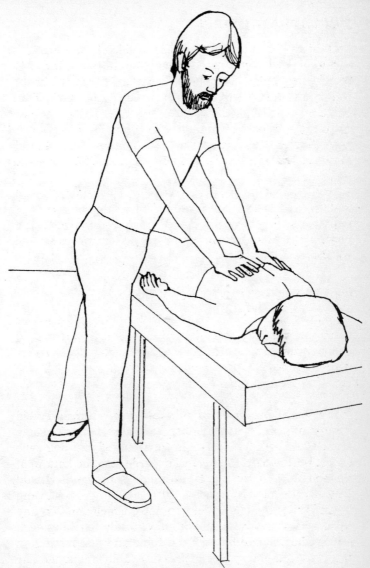

18 Back massage position

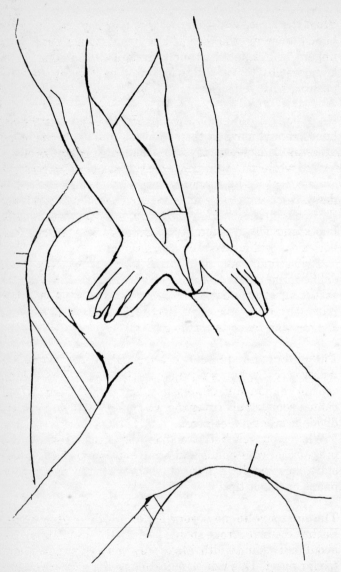

19 Stroking the lower back

Start the first stroke smoothly and gently, moving your hands towards the head. Use your palms (not your fingers, see page 89) to apply the pressure and use your body weight to vary the pressure by leaning, not by pushing with your arms.

Keep your hands moving parallel to each other Both hands should move at the same rate and apply the same pressure. It is very easy to concentrate on the stronger hand and forget the weaker one. Most people are right handed and so the commonest fault is to neglect the left hand. But from the point of view of the person receiving the massage both sides of his or her back are equally important. The discomfort or pain may be on one side but both sides will need similar attention.

If you find your right hand is running away then deliberately concentrate on your left hand. If necessary take your right hand off and just practise with your left hand, or with your right hand if you are left handed. Evenness of touch is very important.

The end of the stroke is determined by your reach. Do not over reach. You will end up off balance and unable to control the amount of pressure you are applying. If you cannot comfortably cover the whole area with one stroke, divide it into smaller areas.

When you reach the end of the stroke release the pressure on your palms and bring your hands back to the start, keeping light contact with the back using your palms or finger tips.

The next stroke move your hands a little further apart. Each successive stroke should overlap the previous one by about half a hand width. Make sure you do not move them too far apart. This can be irritating to the person you are massaging. Each hand should be the same distance from the spine. Carry on until your hands reach the person's sides, then return to the start.

Repeat with greater pressure Continue gradually increasing the pressure each time you return to the start until the pressure is fairly strong.

Stop increasing the pressure when the person you are massaging wants you to, or when you feel there is enough.

Reduce the pressure over successive cycles (in the same way as you increased it) until you are back to your starting pressure. You have now finished massaging this area with this stroke.

Move to the next area if you have not covered all of the lower back; or go on to the next type of stroke. To move to the next area move your feet so that you are positioned opposite the new area. The new area should slightly overlap the previous area.

Kneading

The next stroke is kneading where you use the heel of your hand, not the whole palm as you did in the stroking technique.

The person you massage should be lying in the same position as for the stroking technique. Make sure he or she is lying as close to the edge of the table as possible without feeling unsafe.

Stand facing the buttocks, with your thighs leaning against the edge of the bench or table. Your feet should be side by side, a little apart. You have to apply your body weight to get the necessary pressure without exhausting yourself so it is essential that the height of the table or bench is correct (see page 90).

Place one hand with a little oil on it half way up the
buttocks on the far side of the cleft. Use your stronger
hand first, your right hand if you are right handed, your
left if you are left handed. Rest your other hand on the
back or buttocks.

Applying a slight amount of pressure with only the heel
of your hand, gently slide it away from you towards the
far side. See Drawing 20 below. Each stroke should go as

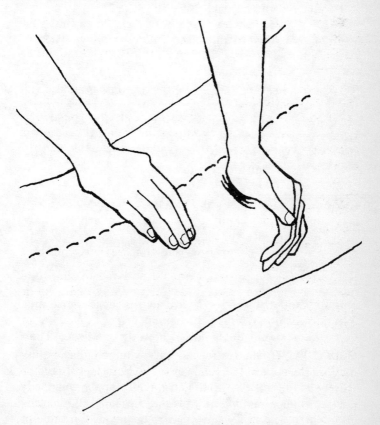

20 Kneading the lower back

far round the buttock as you can reach while maintaining even pressure.

When you have finished the stroke maintain light skin contact while your hand returns to the starting position.

Successive kneading strokes should start about half a hand width further up the back and each should have the same pressure as the previous one. Knead the far buttock and continue up the back kneading the far side of the spine. When you reach so far towards the head that you begin to feel awkward and not in control you have reached your limit.

Return to the start keeping light skin contact and knead again with more pressure. Each time you return to the start, increase the pressure until you or the person you are massaging feel it is strong enough. Then gradually diminish it until you are back at the starting pressure. You have now finished this area.

Move to the next area if you have not kneaded all the lower back. Move your feet so that you are correctly positioned opposite the area you wish to massage. The new area should slightly overlap the previous one. Use more oil when you need to.

Knead the other side To knead the near side move round to the other side of the person, or get him or her to turn round so that the head is where the feet were. Then repeat the above.

Buttock muscles You may find the person you are massaging instinctively tightens up the buttock muscles. Get him or her to relax them. Once aware they are tightening up the person can relax them quickly and easily. This relaxation may have to be repeated several times. There is no point in massaging muscles which are held contracted. You have enough work massaging the muscles which cannot be relaxed without giving yourself more work.

At the waist your strokes should become shorter. This is because the muscles here are the postural muscles. These muscles, which you explored in the touch exercise earlier in this chapter, are not very wide so the length of the stroke will only be an inch or two. You should not apply as much pressure here as you did over the buttocks.

Pressure Bear in mind that everyone has a different tolerance of pressure. What is easily borne by one person can be uncomfortable to someone else. If someone is already in pain they will not be able to put up with a lot of pressure.

If you need to increase the pressure further you can do so by placing the heel of your other hand on the back of the kneading hand. Then apply pressure with the second hand as well as the first. Drawing 21 overleaf shows the left hand positioned to reinforce the right hand.

Use your other hand When you feel confident with your strong hand start kneading with the other one, again resting the non-working hand on the person's back. If you are very right or left handed you may stiffen up. Stop massaging, drop your shoulders, bend your elbows and wrists a little and carry on. The stiffening will go as you get used to massaging.

Both hands can be used to knead the area with each hand working alternately. As one hand finishes its stroke the next one should start its stroke. Each successive

21 Hand to reinforce kneading

stroke should overlap the previous one so that you gradually move up the area. See Drawing 22 opposite.

Deep pressure

This is a powerful technique. It requires greater control and skill than the others and it is essential that you have mastered the earlier skills before using this one.

Stand at the person's side, level with the hips. It does not matter which side, except that you should massage the side furthest from you. Stand so that you are half turned away, facing towards the head. Your feet should be apart with your outside foot pointing towards the head. See Drawing 18 on page 103 on how to stand.

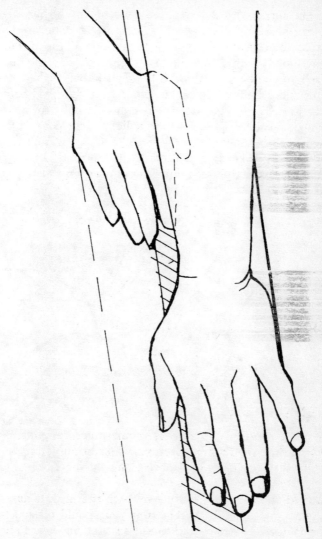

22 Strokes should overlap

Use one hand with the other hand resting on the back. If you are standing on the person's right, use your right thumb, and if on the left your left. Put a small amount of oil on your thumb. Place the pad of the end joint of your thumb on the back just above the cleft between the two buttocks on the far side of the spine. Your thumb should pcint towards the legs, with the rest of your hand towards the head. Your fingers should be lightly clenched with your knuckles touching the skin without any pressure so that your wrist is slightly tilted up at the front. Drawing 23 below shows this technique being used on the upper back.

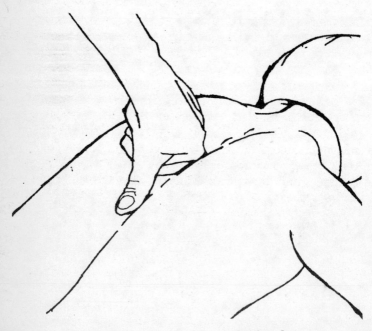

23 Deep pressure on the back

Slowly move your thumb up the back Keep on the middle of the postural muscles so that your thumb is moving parallel to the spine. Use a gentle even pressure. Do not press too hard but keep a smooth and flowing movement. Move your whole body; do not just reach with your arm or bend at the waist. Eventually you will start to stretch. Stop. You have reached the end of the stroke. Return to the starting position keeping a light contact.

Repeat the stroke, this time with a little more pressure. Continue applying more pressure each time until you or the person you are massaging feel that there is enough pressure. Then start to reduce the pressure on successive strokes until you return to the starting pressure.

Massage the other side Move your thumb so that it lies on the near side of the spine and repeat the above. The person does not need to change position.

Reinforce your thumb

You can only exert a small amount of pressure using your thumb by itself. If you press too hard your thumb will feel uncomfortable. The next stage is to use your other hand to reinforce your thumb. Only do this when you are quite confident and fluent with using your thumb alone.

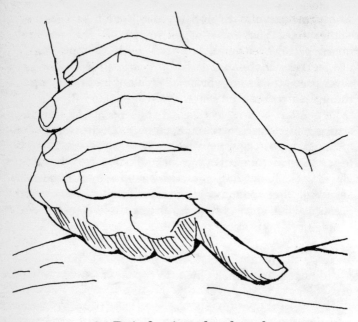

24 Reinforcing the thumb

Assuming your right hand is doing the massage, it should be in the position described above. Place your left hand on the back of your right thumb so that the little finger end of the heel of the left hand rests on the nail of the right thumb. You will find that the rest of the heel of your left hand rests comfortably along the shaft of the right thumb. See Drawing 24 above.

Lean with your left hand onto the thumb of your right hand. This way you can exert a lot of pressure. Your right thumb becomes a sensitive tool. The position should of course be reversed if you are using your left hand reinforced with your right hand.

The pressure of the initial strokes should be light and comfortable. They should not move off the postural muscles. However you will quickly reach as much pressure as can be tolerated, so increase the pressure of successive strokes very gradually. Then gradually reduce the pressure over successive strokes.

Remember to keep the pressure even throughout the stroke. The tendency is to start off light because you begin too close to yourself. Then you get stronger as your stance becomes more comfortable, followed by an easing off as you start to stretch. There is also a tendency to slip sideways off the postural muscles. This could hurt so treat it seriously. The solution is careful practice.

Pelvic rim

In the touch exercise you did earlier you followed the rim of the pelvis with your finger. You can apply the deep pressure technique along this rim. The warnings about pressure and slipping apply just as strongly here, but if you can use this technique it is very useful for aches in the lower back. The big muscles which run down the back eventually attach to the pelvis along this rim. Aches and pains in this area often involve these muscles and where they join the bone.

Stand facing the buttocks Place your reinforced thumb with a small amount of oil on it at the top of the buttock cleft on the far side of the spine. Now slowly move your thumb up the back, but this time find and follow the pelvic rim as it curves away from you. When the rim curves downwards towards the table you have reached the end of your stroke. You may have to practise before you can follow the rim without losing your way but it is worth the effort. As before, gradually increase the pressure and then decrease it over successive strokes.

To massage the near side move round to the other side of the person, or get him or her to turn round so that the head is where the feet were. Then repeat the above.

9
Upper back massage

People all over the world suffer from discomfort in the upper part of the back. The commonest areas are between the shoulder blades, around the shoulders and at the base of the neck. Typical symptoms include aching, tightness and stiffness. Headaches due to muscle tension, burning sensations in the neck and shoulders as well as tingling and numbness in the arms and hands can come from the upper back. These symptoms can also stem from trouble in the neck. Massaging the neck is dealt with in the next chapter.

If the person you are massaging has aches, pain or discomfort in the upper back which you hope to alleviate, get a proper diagnosis. Although the discomfort may be simply muscular, do not take the risk of assuming this. Consult a GP, qualified osteopath or physiotherapist first.

This chapter describes massaging the back from just below the bottom of the shoulder blades to the base of the neck. If you have already read and used chapter 8 on low back massage, treat this chapter as following on from that.

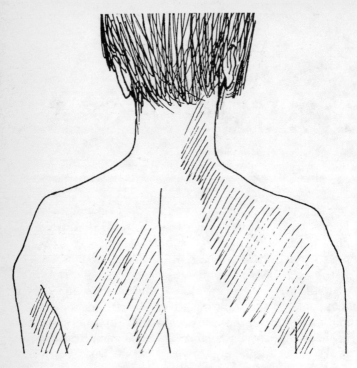

25 Upper back (surface)

Look at Drawings 25 and 26 (above). Drawing 25 shows the upper back as you see it. The right side of Drawing 26 shows the muscles which lie just under the skin, while the left side shows a deeper layer together with the shoulder blade and some ribs. If you can get a mental picture of how the muscles flow under the skin, the massage will be much more effective. To help you familiarise yourself with the area, start with an exercise to show you what is where.

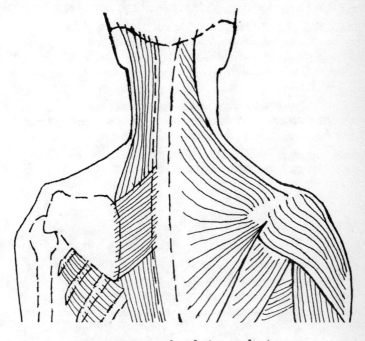

26 Upper back (muscles)

Position

The person you massage should lie face downwards. The head should be turned towards you. If that is uncomfortable it can be turned to the other side or the forehead can rest on the hands. It is important that the person you massage is comfortable. Massaging someone who is uncomfortable and therefore holding him or herself tense is a waste of time. You have enough work massaging the tension which cannot be helped.

The arms should be relaxed. If possible, they should

hang over the edge of the table, although that will depend on what he or she is lying on. Otherwise they can be at the sides. If necessary they may be supporting the forehead.

The back should be uncovered. There is no point massaging through clothes and if only a small part is uncovered you will become frustrated trying to avoid getting oil on the clothes. If you are massaging a man ask him to take his top clothes off so that he is undressed from the waist upwards. If you are massaging a woman ask her to remove all her upper clothes except her bra which you should undo when she is lying down. If her bra fastens at the front ask her to undo it when she is already lying down.

Touch exercise

Stand opposite the base of the neck. With a little oil on your index finger put it on the middle of the base of the neck so that you are touching the spine. You should feel the bone. If you do not, move your finger around a little until you do. Although it can be hard to see the outline of the spine on well covered people, it is usually not difficult to feel it here.

Run your finger slowly down the spine towards the bottom of the back. There is no need to use much pressure. You are trying to feel what is under your finger and the more pressure you use the less you feel. Note that there are alternating bumps and gaps as you move your finger down the spine. The bumps are the tips of the individual bones or vertebrae of the spine.

Shoulder

Go back to the base of the neck. Move your finger away from the spine along the top of the shoulder towards you. Eventually you will reach the end which is hard and bony.

This is the top of the shoulder joint.

Move back towards the neck. Note that the area is soft under your finger. It is muscle and not bone. If there is a lot of tension in the area the muscle will feel tight and knotted. It sometimes feels as though there are bits of rope under the skin. If you can detect this the area certainly needs some massage.

Repeat this, exploring the other shoulder.

Shoulder blade

Put your finger half way along the near shoulder and then move it down the back for about an inch. Initially you move over muscle but you will soon come to a hard bony ridge. This is the upper edge of the shoulder blade, the scapula, which is roughly triangular, with the pointed end at the bottom and the flat end at the top. The ridge runs roughly parallel with the shoulder.

Follow the ridge of the shoulder blade towards you. The outer end finishes at the shoulder joint. Then move your finger to the inner end. It suddenly stops when it meets another ridge running down the back. This is the inner edge of the shoulder blade.

Continue down the inner edge carefully Run your finger up and down until you are satisfied that you can follow its entire length. If the person is lying with arms over the edge, or with forehead resting on the hands, then it will run outwards and downwards. If the arms are by the side it will run more or less parallel to the spine.

When you reach the bottom it will suddenly turn outwards and start going back up and out towards the side. There is no need to follow it any further.

If the person you are exploring is very thin you can discover the inner edge fairly easily and you may be able to see the outline of the shoulder blade. If he or she has more flesh or is muscular you might have to concentrate quite hard. Please persist. This area is almost always involved in neck, shoulder and upper back ache. Since you may massage it frequently it pays to familiarise yourself with it.

Repeat with the other shoulder blade, following the top of the ridge and down the inner edge.

Muscles

The next area to explore is between the inner edge of the shoulder blade and the spine. There are two groups of muscles in this area, the postural muscles and the muscles connecting the spine to the shoulder blade.

Postural muscles Look at the back. On either side of the spine there is a raised area about an inch wide running the length of the back. If you are not sure put your finger on the spine and slowly move it outwards. After you move off the bone of the spine, you will feel the softer texture of muscles.

Moving your finger across these muscles you discover they are not flat but rise up a bit and then go lower until they seem to end. These are the postural muscles which keep your spine straight.

They run from the bottom of the back right up to the base of the skull. Follow them with your finger. They are easier to see in someone who has well developed muscles, but we all have them and they are often involved in back discomfort. They are shown on the left side of Drawing 26 on page 119.

Explore the postural muscles on both sides of the spine.

Muscles connecting the shoulder blade to the spine
These muscles are often the cause of much discomfort so

familiarise yourself with them. Look at the left side of Drawing 26 on page 119. You can see them going upwards and inwards from the inner edge of the shoulder blade to the spine.

These muscles may be a little difficult to see or feel although it is easier in people with well developed muscles. One place where they are often easy to feel is at the top inner edge of the shoulder blade. If you put your finger there you almost always detect the knotty feel of tense contracted muscles. Be careful. This area can be very tender and although it will benefit from massage do not be too heavy. You will not cause any harm but it could be very painful.

Explore these muscles on both sides of the spine.

Ribs

Crossing the upper back are the ribs. They run sideways from the spine rather like the hoops of a barrel. They actually start off at the spine but this is too far beneath the surface for you to see or feel. They run sideways under the muscles you have just explored. They then continue under the shoulder blade, round the side and into the front. The ribs finally join up with the breast bone in the middle of the front of the chest.

Put your finger halfway between the spine and the inner edge of the shoulder blade Move it up and down the back an inch or so. You should be able to feel the ribs as your fingers cross them. You may have to press firmly. This will depend partly on the person's build. The ribs are easier to find on a thin person. Quite apart from whether they are fat, big framed people have greater muscle covering than smaller framed people and this makes it harder to follow their bones. It is easier if the arms are hanging over the side.

When you have found the ribs slide your finger with a little oil on it off one rib so that it rests in the groove between the rib and the next one.

Move your finger along that groove away from the spine. You will soon meet the shoulder blade.

Start off again below the shoulder blade. This time see how far round you can follow the ribs. On most people they initially go downwards towards the feet and then curve upwards as they go round the side to the front.

Explore the ribs on both sides of the spine.

You need to be familiar with the area you are massaging to be effective. This touch exercise will help you. Do it several times until you are happy with it. Also refer to Drawing 26 on page 119 to improve your mental picture of what lies under your hands.

Stroking the upper back

The person you massage should be lying face down as described earlier in this chapter. He or she should lie as close to you as possible without feeling unsafe. Stand at the side a little below the area you are going to massage and half turn towards the head. It does not matter which side you are standing.

Your feet should be apart. If you are standing on the person's right your right foot should be in front and pointing towards the head. Similarly if you are on the left your left foot should be in front and pointed towards the head. You should be touching the bench or table with your thigh.

Put a small amount of oil onto your hands Avoid using too much. Later when this has been absorbed take some more. Rest your hands on the back just below the shoulder blades a little in front of you with one hand on

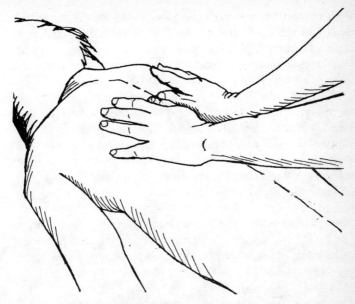

27 Stroking the upper back

each side of the spine. Your fingers should point towards the head with your thumbs almost touching. See above.

Move your hands slowly up towards the top of the back using your palms to apply gentle pressure. Use the palms of your hands to apply pressure, not your fingers and thumbs (see page 89). Do not worry if your fingers or thumbs are touching the skin. They should be but without any pressure.

Keep both hands moving together and parallel with each other. Make sure both hands apply the same amount of pressure. If you find it hard at first, try using one hand at a time. You may need to practise with only your weak hand until you feel comfortable, especially if you are very right or left-handed.

The distance covered with each stroke depends on you. Do not go further than is comfortable. When you start to stretch you have come to the end of the stroke. If you carry on further you will be unable to maintain an even pressure and might lose your balance.

When you have finished the stroke do not take your hands off. It is better to maintain some contact. If you remove your hands between strokes the person you are massaging may find it unpleasant. Return your hands to the starting position keeping your fingers lightly touching the back.

The next stroke your hands should be half a hand width further apart so that the new stroke overlaps the previous one. Your hands should still move together in the same direction and with the same amount of pressure.

On subsequent strokes continue to increase the separation between your hands, moving half a hand width each time. As you increase the distance between your hands you will find that they eventually reach the person's sides. You have gone far enough. Go back to the centre keeping light skin contact.

Restart at the centre with more pressure Repeat this process several times, each time increasing the pressure a little. Stop when you are applying as much pressure as the person can comfortably tolerate or you feel is strong enough.

Then gradually reduce the pressure each time in the same way you built it up until you return to the starting pressure. You have now finished this area.

If you have not reached the neck repeat this sequence,

standing higher up just below the next area you wish to massage. Start your stroke just below where you finished it last time. Move progressively up the back until you reach the neck, then move on to the next stroke or another area.

Kneading

The next type of massage is kneading where you use only the heel of your hand, not the whole palm as you did in the stroking technique.

The person you massage should lie in the same position as for the stroking technique. Make sure he or she is lying as close to the edge of the table as possible without feeling unsafe.

Stand facing the area to be massaged, with your thighs leaning against the edge of the table. Your feet should be side by side, a little apart. You have to be able to apply your body weight to get the necessary pressure without exhausting yourself, so it is essential that the height of the table or bench is correct (see page 90).

Kneading the postural muscles

When you knead the postural muscles, you massage across their width. You explored the postural muscles in the touch exercise earlier in this chapter.

Put your hand on the back just beyond the spine and below the shoulder blades with a small amount of oil in it. Use your stronger hand: your right hand if you are right-handed, your left if you are left-handed. You will use your other hand later but for now rest it on the back.

Applying slight pressure with the heel of your hand, with your fingers resting on the person's back, gently slide

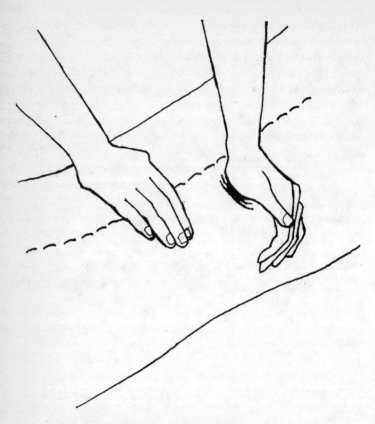

28 Kneading the upper back

your hand away from you towards the person's far side. See Drawing 28 above.

Return to where you started, keeping your hand lightly in contact with the skin.

Successive strokes should start half a hand width further up the back and should have the same pressure as the previous stroke. Eventually you will feel awkward as you lean further sideways. Stop and go back to where you started keeping light skin contact.

Massage with greater pressure Repeat this procedure applying a little more pressure each time you go back to the start until you or the person you are massaging feel there is enough pressure.

Gradually reduce the pressure in the same way as you built it up. When you return to the pressure you started with you have finished that particular area.

If you have not reached the neck move your feet so that you stand opposite the new area. Don't stretch. Start again. Make sure that the start of the new area overlaps the end of the old one.

Knead the near side Go round to the other side of the person or ask him or her to turn round so that the feet are where the head was.

Use your other hand When you feel confident with your strong hand start kneading with the other one, resting your non-working hand on the back. If you are very right or left handed you may start to stiffen up. Stop massaging, drop your shoulders, bend your elbows and wrists a little and carry on. The stiffness will go as you get used to massaging and your confidence improves.

Both hands When you are happy kneading with either hand use each hand for alternate strokes. Start off with one hand, say your left. As it gets towards the end of its stroke your right hand should start its stroke while you remove the left hand. Successive strokes should overlap by half a hand width. It is a good idea to turn the first

hand outwards slightly as it reaches the end of its stroke.
This makes room for the second one to come in.

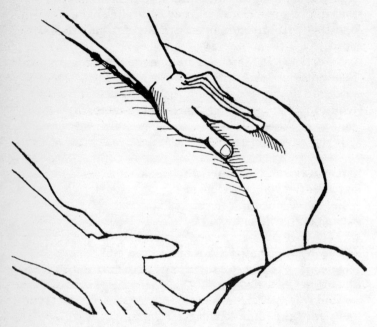

29 Thumb kneading the upper back

Use your thumb Another way of kneading the postural
muscles, especially if you have big hands and the person
you are massaging is small, is to apply pressure with your
thumb instead of the heel of your hand.

With a small amount of oil on your thumb, put it on the
person's back just beyond the spine. It does not matter
which hand you are using. Then, exerting pressure slide
your thumb across the postural muscles towards your
fingers. See Drawing 29 above.

Having completed the stroke move your thumb a little way up towards the person's head, maintaining slight skin contact, and repeat. Make sure this stroke overlaps the previous one slightly. After several strokes you will find that you are leaning sideways towards the person's head.

Return to the start maintaining light skin contact. Repeat the routine with more pressure. Each time you return to the start increase the pressure until it reaches a comfortable maximum. Then reduce the pressure in the same way as you built it up.

If you have not reached the neck move your feet so that you stand opposite the new area rather than stretching. Start again. Make sure that the start of the new area overlaps the end of the old one.

Reinforce your thumb When you have got the hang of it you can increase the pressure by placing the heel of your other hand on the back of your thumb.

Assuming your right hand is doing the massage place the heel of your left hand on the back of the right thumb so that the little finger end of the heel of your left hand rests on the nail of your right thumb. You will find the rest of the heel of your left hand rests comfortably along the shaft of the right thumb. See Drawing 30 overleaf.

Apply pressure by leaning with your left hand onto the thumb of your right hand. This way you can exert a lot of pressure. Your right thumb becomes a sensitive tool. This is not the same as deep pressure, which is described later in this chapter.

The position should of course be reversed if you are using the left hand reinforced with the right hand.

Kneading the shoulders

Some areas are hard to knead using the heel of your hand

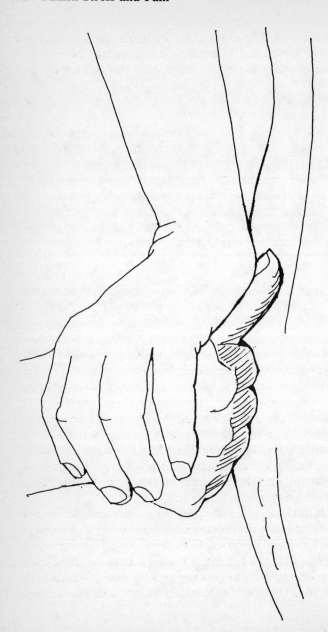

30 Reinforcing the thumb

or your thumb. The tops of the shoulders are a particular
example. If you try kneading them as described above
your hands may slip off. There are two other methods:

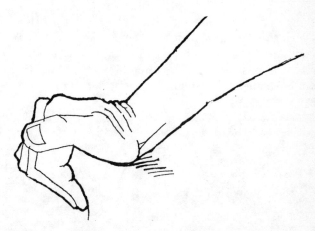

31 Kneading the shoulders

**Knead between the heel of your hand and your
fingers** If you stand on the person's right, use your right
hand to massage the left (far) shoulder and vice versa. If
you were to use your left hand you would find that when
you reach the neck your thumb gets in the way.

Stand a little behind your hands with your other hand
resting on the back. The person's head should be turned
towards you and the far arm should be by the side. This
gives you good access to the shoulder.

Look at Drawing 31 above. Your fingers and the heel of
your hand are either side of the muscle to be kneaded.
You are going to move the heel of your hand towards your
fingers so that the muscle is kneaded between the two.

Do not move your fingers towards the heel of your hand.
You will pinch the flesh which hurts, and you cannot

apply any degree of pressure. As always you must apply
pressure by using your body weight. If you are squeezing
with your fingers you cannot boost the pressure with your
body weight.

If you need to increase the pressure further you can do
so by placing the heel of your other hand on the back of
the kneading hand. Then apply pressure with the second
hand as well as the first. Drawing 32 below shows the left
hand positioned to reinforce the right hand.

32 Hand to reinforce kneading

Knead thumb to forefingers This other method to
knead the shoulders may be easier if the person you are
massaging is small. You and the person should remain in

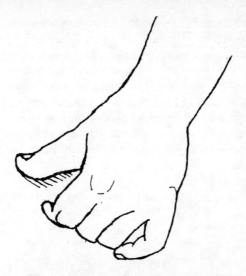

33 Thumb kneading the shoulders

the same position as described above. If you are standing on the person's right, use your left hand to massage the left (far) shoulder. If you are standing on the person's left use your right hand for the right (far) shoulder. The other hand should rest gently on the surface of the person's back.

Put your massaging hand on the person's shoulder nearly at the tip with your thumb on the back of the shoulder. Your index finger should be placed under the front of the shoulder so that the shoulder muscle lies between your thumb and index finger. Now, keeping your finger where it is, move your thumb towards it exerting a small amount of pressure so that the muscle is squeezed between the thumb and finger. Avoid pinching the skin. See Drawing 33 above.

To apply greater pressure you can place the heel of your

other hand on your thumb in the same way as you did in the thumb stroke above.

Using either of the above techniques, start at the top of the shoulder and work towards the neck. You need a little oil on your hand or thumb. Do not start in the middle of the shoulder and work one way and then the other. If the flow of massage is consistently in one direction the person receiving it will relax more easily than if you keep changing.

Successive strokes should overlap When you have reached the neck, go back to the tip of the shoulder, keeping a light skin contact. Start again with greater pressure. Repeat this each time, gradually increasing the pressure. This area is rather sensitive to pressure so increase the pressure slowly. Stop when either of you feels that you are applying enough pressure.

Gradually reduce the pressure in the same way as you built it up. When you have returned to the starting pressure you have finished this area.

Massage the other shoulder Go round to the other side of the person or ask the person to turn round so that the head is where the feet were. You could knead the near side using your other hand but it is rather awkward and if you need to apply any degree of pressure you may find it difficult. For this reason avoid using both hands simultaneously.

Sitting You can massage the shoulders with the person sitting. Stand behind the person, who can sit up or lean forward with his or her arms on a table and head resting on the forearms.

Use both hands at once, one on each shoulder. If you are kneading between the heel of your hand and your fingers

you may find that when you get to the neck your thumbs
get in the way. The alternative is to knead between your
thumb and fingers.

Make sure that both hands are applying the same
pressure and are moving in a co-ordinated manner from
the tip of the shoulder towards the neck. It is very easy for
your strong hand to be working away while the weaker
one, usually the left, is doing very little. If you find that is
happening, practise using only the weak hand.

Deep pressure on the postural muscles

This is a very useful method of massaging the postural
muscles. You can apply a lot of pressure but be careful. It
is easy to use too much. Start as low down the back as you
wish and go up as far as the start of the neck.

Stand at the person's side, a little below the area you
intend to massage. It does not matter which side.

Half turn towards the head with your outside foot in
front and your toes pointing towards the head. Make sure
that the person is close to you without feeling too near the
edge. Your side should touch the bench or table. You
cannot be too close to the person you are massaging, it
makes your task much easier.

Put the front pad of the end joint of your thumb on
the person's back just the far side of the spine at the
bottom of the area you wish to massage. If you are
standing on the person's right, use your right thumb; if on
the left, use your left thumb. You need a small amount of
oil on your thumb. The thumb should be pointing towards
the person's legs, with the rest of the hand towards the
head. Your fingers should be lightly clenched and your
knuckles touching the skin without any pressure so that

your wrist is slightly tilted up at the front. See Drawing 34 below.

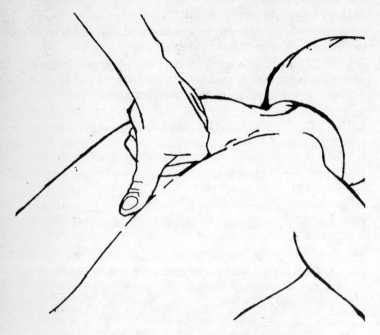

34 Deep pressure on the back

Slowly move your thumb up the back using a gentle even pressure. The thumb should keep on the postural muscles and parallel to the spine. Do not press too hard but keep a smooth and flowing movement. Move your whole trunk. Do not just reach with your arm or bend at the waist. Eventually you will start to stretch. You have reached the end of the stroke. Return to the starting position keeping a light contact.

Repeat the movement, this time with a little more pressure. Each time you return to the starting position, increase the pressure a little. After a few strokes you will find that you are applying all the pressure your thumb can cope with. To apply more use your other hand to reinforce your thumb as described below.

When you or the person you are massaging feel there is enough pressure stop.

Gradually reduce the pressure on successive strokes in the same way as you built it up until you return to the starting pressure.

Continue to massage the rest of the upper back up to the neck if you have not already reached it. When you have finished massaging the postural muscles on the far side of the spine, apply deep pressure on the near side in the same way.

Reinforce your thumb

You can only exert a small amount of pressure using your thumb by itself. If you press too hard your thumb will start to feel uncomfortable. The next stage is to use your other hand to reinforce your thumb. Only do this when you are confident and fluent using your thumb alone.

Assuming your right hand is doing the massage, it should be in the position described above. Place your left hand on the back of your right thumb so that the little finger end of the heel of your left hand rests on the nail of your right thumb. You will find that the rest of the heel of your left hand rests comfortably along the shaft of the right thumb. See Drawing 30 on page 132.

Lean with your left hand onto the thumb of your right hand This way you can exert a lot of pressure. The position should of course be reversed if you are using your left hand reinforced with your right hand.

Pressure The strokes should maintain the same path and not move off the postural muscles. The pressure of the initial strokes should be light and comfortable. You will soon reach as much pressure as can be tolerated so increase the pressure of successive strokes very gradually. Then gradually reduce the pressure over successive strokes.

Remember to keep the pressure even throughout the stroke. The tendency is to start off light because you begin too close to yourself. Then you get stronger as your stance becomes more comfortable, followed by an easing off as you start to stretch. There is also a tendency to slip sideways off the postural muscles.

Deep pressure on the shoulder blade

The deep pressure technique is especially useful for the shoulder blade. A lot of the muscles contributing to neck and shoulder pain originate from this area. However, the area is often painful and the person you are massaging may not be able to handle the amount of pressure you used on the postural muscles. Increase the pressure more slowly here.

Stand on the opposite side to the shoulder blade you will massage. If you are massaging the person's right side, stand on his or her left side.

Use either hand here. If you use your left hand, position it as shown in Drawing 34 on page 138, with your thumb pointing towards the leg. If you use your right hand, position it as shown in Drawing 35 opposite with your thumb pointing towards the head. Use whichever position you find easiest.

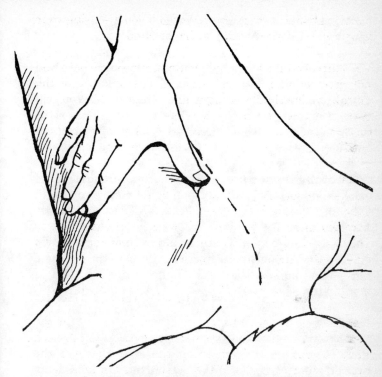

35 Deep pressure on the shoulder blade

Start at the bottom of the inner edge of the shoulder blade Work upwards along this edge staying on it. You may find it takes quite a bit of concentration to keep on it, especially if the person you are massaging is well covered.

When you reach the top of this edge move your thumb away from yourself along the top of the shoulder blade towards the far side. When you reach the far end stop and return to where you started, maintaining light skin contact.

Repeat the movement, this time with a little more pressure. Each time you return to the starting position, increase the pressure a little. After a few strokes you will find that you are applying all the pressure that your thumb can cope with. To apply more pressure use your other hand to reinforce your thumb. This was described on page 139.

When you or the person you are massaging feel there is enough pressure stop.

Gradually reduce the pressure on successive strokes in the same way as you built it up until you return to the starting pressure.

Massage the other shoulder blade Stand on the other side of the person, either by going round to the other side or getting him or her to turn round so that the feet are where the head was.

10
Neck massage

Many aches and pains are found in the neck itself although the effects of neck trouble can be felt in your arms, hands or even fingers. The neck can feel tight or stiff. You may find you cannot turn round as far as you should. You notice this when reversing the car or looking over your shoulder.

Other symptoms include aches, pain and tightness in your shoulders, and a pins-and-needles sensation in your hands or fingers. A very common result of neck trouble is headache. These symptoms are often caused by muscular tension and can be helped by massage. However they may have other causes. Get a doctor, qualified osteopath or physiotherapist to check before you start any massage.

Chapter 9 dealt with massaging the upper back, and stopped at the base of the neck. This chapter goes from there to the base of the skull.

Clothes

The person you are massaging should be unclothed from the shoulders upwards. Although you are massaging the neck many of your strokes will start around the shoulders. In practice it is easiest if the back is bare. If you are

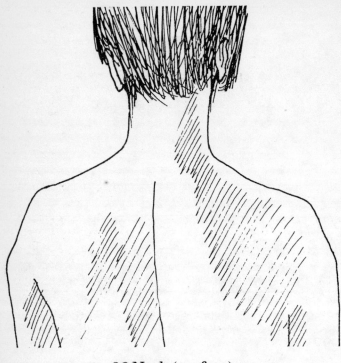

36 Neck (surface)

massaging a woman there is no need to remove the bra but you should ask her to slip the straps off her shoulders.

Position

The person you massage should lie face downwards. The arms should be resting in front with the forehead on the forearms. Lift long hair out of your way or hold it up with clips or a hair band. Since you are massaging right up to the base of the skull some disruption of the hairstyle will be inevitable.

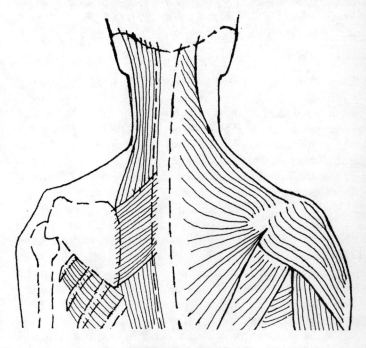

37 Neck (muscles)

Touch exercise

Look at Drawing 36. This shows the neck as you see it. Drawing 37 next to it shows some of the muscles and bones which lie beneath the skin. The right side shows the muscles just under the skin, while the left side shows a deeper layer of muscles.

It is important you develop a mental picture of what is under your hands when you massage. The greater your familiarity with the area the more effective your massage will be. To help you relate what you feel with your fingers to the anatomy of the area, start off with a simple touch exercise.

The neck

Stand at the side (it does not matter which side) so you are level with the top of the shoulders. Put your index finger with small amount of oil on it on the middle of the back of the neck at shoulder level. You should feel the hard bone of the spine. If you do not, move your finger around until you do.

Use the index finger of your strong hand since this has the most sensitivity. Your strong hand is your right hand if you are right handed, left if you are left handed.

Slowly move your index finger up the neck keeping it on the bone. Initially you will feel knobs of bone with gaps between them. These knobs are the tips of the vertebrae of the spine. Further up the neck they get closer together and it becomes more difficult to distinguish the individual bones. If you cannot tell where one ends and the next begins don't worry.

Do not press hard. A light touch makes it easier to feel and if the person has a neck problem it may be very painful if you press too hard.

When you have nearly reached the skull the knobs may seem to disappear. This is because the spine curves inwards at this point, making it hard to feel.

Head

When you reach the top of the spine you will meet a ridge of bone. It runs at right angles to the spine across the top of the neck. This is the base of the skull. This ridge runs round the bottom of the head like the hoop of a barrel and you should follow it until it ends just behind the ears.

It may not be so obvious to the touch when your finger

moves away from the centre towards the sides but you can still follow it. There is usually hair growing here which makes feeling the ridge a bit harder but persevere. A lot of the muscles in the neck start from this ridge and it often needs massaging.

Muscles

Return to the base of the neck and put your index finger with a small amount of oil on it, back on the spine. Move your finger very slowly towards one side of the spine. It does not matter which side. Your finger will go into a narrow trough and then on to a soft ridge running parallel to the spine. This ridge is made of the muscles which hold your head up and is a continuation of the postural muscles discussed in chapters 8 and 9 on low and upper back massage.

Put your finger on this ridge and ask the person to slightly lift up his or her head just a couple of inches. You will feel this ridge go from being firm but soft to being taut like a rope under tension. Now ask the person to lower the head so that he or she is completely relaxed and note how the ridge returns to its softer state.

Next ask the person to turn his or her head towards you and put the arms by the sides. Repeat the above exercise in this position. Although it is more difficult to feel the ridge in this position it is often a more comfortable position for the person receiving the massage.

Stroking the neck

The person you massage should lie on his or her front with the head face down resting on the forehead or else turned towards you. The arms can be by the side although if lying with the forehead down he or she may want to rest it on one or both forearms.

Stand at the person's side about six inches below the level of the shoulders so that he or she is on the side of your stronger hand. You should be facing towards the person's head, with your outer foot in front pointing towards the person's head.

Put a little oil in your hand nearer the person. Place your palm (see page 89) on the base of the neck just the far side of the spine. Your fingers should be pointing towards the head without exerting any pressure.

Gently slide your hand up the neck until your palm reaches the base of the skull. Keep your palm parallel to the spine. The pressure you exert should be firm but gentle. On completion of the stroke return to the base of the neck maintaining a light skin contact.

Repeat with greater pressure Continue increasing the pressure with each stroke until either of you feels that you are applying enough pressure.

Gradually reduce the pressure with successive strokes until you are back at the start.

Massage the other side of the neck Go round to the other side of the person or get him or her to turn round so that the head is where the feet were. Then use your other hand to massage the other side of the neck in the same way as before.

Thumb stroke

Another method of stroking the neck is to use your thumb. Put a small amount of oil on your hand nearer the person. Place your hand on the neck so that your thumb lies on the near side of the neck and your forefinger on the

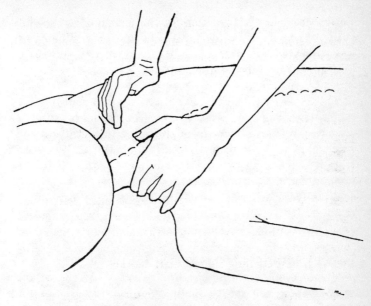

38 Thumb stroking the neck

far side. Your other hand should rest on the person's shoulder or on the surface above the shoulder. See Drawing 38 above.

Slowly slide your thumb up the side of the neck. Start at the base of the neck and continue to the base of the skull. Use firm but gentle pressure keeping it even from start to finish. Use just the front pad of the thumb. The rest of your hand should slide upwards without pressing. Be careful your fingers do not touch the front of the neck. It will feel uncomfortable even if there is no pressure. Although there are muscles in the front of the neck, massage must be confined to the back and side.

The first stroke starts immediately adjacent to the

spine. Maintain that position for the length of the stroke with your thumb moving parallel to the spine. When you have reached the base of the skull return to the start position maintaining a light contact.

Successive strokes The next stroke starts about half an inch away from the spine towards your side and successive strokes move away from the spine in increments of half an inch. As you do this, although the pad of your thumb is doing the work, the rest of the thumb should keep in contact with the skin.

When your stroke ends half way between the person's spine and ear you have gone far enough. Return to the start maintaining light contact.

Repeat with greater pressure Increase the pressure each time you return to the start. Eventually either you or the person you are massaging will feel there is enough pressure.

Reduce pressure with successive series of strokes until you have returned to the starting pressure.

Massage the other side of the neck To do this you have three choices. The first is to go round to the other side of the person or to get him or her to turn round so that the head is where the feet were. Use your other palm or thumb to massage in the same way as before.

The second is to maintain the same position but use your index finger to massage the far side of the neck. It is difficult to apply as much pressure this way because you cannot lean onto your finger in the same way that you can lean onto your thumb.

The third is to maintain the same position but this time use your other hand, reaching over the neck and again using your thumb. This can be quite awkward because

you need to twist quite a lot but you can apply pressure if
necessary.

Thumb kneading

Stand in the same position as for the thumb stroking, with
the person you are massaging lying face downwards with
the forehead resting either on the surface or on the
forearms.

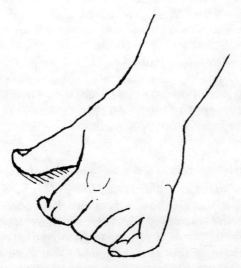

39 Thumb kneading the neck

Use your hand nearer the person, with your other
hand resting on the near shoulder or on the surface. Put
your hand on the person's far shoulder at the base of the
neck so that your thumb is just the far side of the spine.
Your index finger should be placed under the front of the
shoulder so that the shoulder muscle lies between the
thumb and index finger.

Keeping your finger where it is, move your thumb towards it while exerting a small amount of pressure so that the muscle is squeezed between sides of the thumb and finger. Avoid pinching. See Drawing 39 above.

Move your thumb and finger half an inch up the neck and repeat. Carry on until you reach the base of the skull. Return to the start position keeping a light contact and repeat with more pressure. Continue doing this, increasing the pressure each time, until either of you feels there is enough pressure. Then gradually reduce it until you have returned to the starting pressure.

Knead the near side of the neck with this method using your other hand. If you find it awkward and difficult to apply any degree of pressure, go round to the other side or ask the person to turn round, so that the head is where the feet were, and repeat with your other hand.

Heel kneading

Another method of kneading is to use the heel of the hand instead of the thumb. This is particularly useful if the person you are massaging has big neck muscles or you have very small hands. If you are massaging the person's left side stand on his or her right and use your right hand.

Place the heel of your hand with a little oil on it in the same place as you put your thumb, with three or four fingers resting on the front side of the muscle. Without moving your fingers slide the heel towards them so that the muscle gets squeezed between the two. See Drawing 40 opposite.

Be careful not to dig your finger tips into the flesh. Also avoid moving your fingers towards the heel of your hand. As with most massage strokes you use your body weight

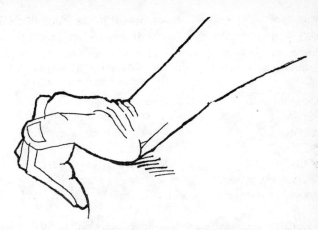

40 Heel kneading the neck

to apply the pressure and this can only be done here with the heel of your hand and not your fingers.

The next stroke starts a little further up the neck, slightly overlapping the previous one. Continue massaging further up the neck with successive strokes until you reach the skull. Return to the start position keeping skin contact and repeat with more pressure. Continue doing this, increasing the pressure each time. Then gradually reduce the pressure each time until you return to the starting pressure.

Knead the other side Either go round to the other side or get the person to turn so that the feet are where the head was. Then repeat with your other hand.

Base of skull

The other area needing massage is the ridge of bone at the base of the skull. This is where a lot of neck muscles start, so you can often help neck trouble from here. Ask the person to lie face down with the forehead resting on the hands or forearms.

Stand level with the shoulders, facing towards the head, so that he or she is on the side of your stronger hand.

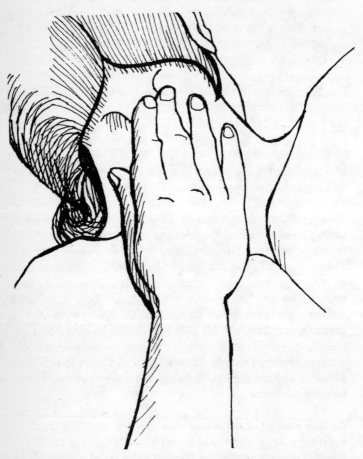

41 Massage the base of the skull

Find the ridge of bone at the base of the skull at the top of the spine. Put the top front pad of the middle finger of your stronger hand onto it so that you are pressing upwards onto the underside of the ridge. Do not use any oil.

Rest your other hand on the surface or lightly on top of the person's head. Without sliding your finger over the skin move it in very small circles so that the skin is moving with the finger. See Drawing 41 opposite.

The skin is slightly loose all over the body and you can move it a small amount before the finger starts to slide. If you are not sure, try doing it on your own hand first. Without using any oil, either on your finger or your hand, put your finger lightly on the back of your hand. Move it back and forth by an eighth of an inch or so without sliding it over the skin. You will see that the skin moves with your finger until you try to move too far. Then your finger starts to slide over the skin.

Massage along the ridge at the base of the skull, using very small circular movements without sliding over the skin. Do three circles using light but definite pressure. Then remove the pressure and slide your finger on half an inch away from you, maintaining light contact, and repeat.

Carry on until you have reached the back of the person's ear. The last bit of the ridge sticks down further than the rest. You will probably feel the tight band of a tendon coming from it. Do not massage very hard here and if there are signs of tenderness leave it alone. It can be very sensitive.

At the end of the ridge return to the starting position keeping a light contact and repeat with greater pressure. Each time you return to the starting point increase the pressure until either you or the person feel that there is enough.

Then gradually reduce the pressure until you are back at the starting point.

Other side of the ridge You may be able to massage it without changing position. Otherwise go round to the other side or get the person to turn so the head is where the feet were and use your other hand.

Shoulders and the back

When you give the neck a massage it is a good idea to massage the shoulders as well. In fact massaging the shoulders can naturally lead to massaging the neck. The ways of massaging the upper back and shoulders are covered in chapter 9.

If you also used chapter 8 massaging the lower part of the back, start to combine these three chapters to give a massage along the whole of the back.

Massage always starts off with stroking and the kneading comes later. When you massage the whole of the back you should stroke the whole of the back first and then knead. As with all skills, practice is the main requirement once you have grasped the basics. The more you massage the more at ease and fluent you become. You will learn more if you massage different people. People's bodies vary considerably and learning to adapt your technique to these differences will increase your skill.

11
Leg massage

A lot of discomfort in the leg comes from muscular strains, often after exertion or sporting activity. Typical symptoms are localised aches or more severe pain. Discomfort can also come from fractures and varicose veins. Symptoms such as numbness or pins and needles may stem from trouble in the back. So before you massage somebody's legs consult a doctor, qualified osteopath or physiotherapist if the person is in pain.

Varicose veins

These are often found on people's legs. It is usually safe to massage around varicose veins but can be dangerous to massage over them. If they are large or painful see a doctor first.

Clothes

The person you massage should be undressed from the waist downwards except for briefs or knickers. If the person feels embarrassed put a towel over the pelvic area but the legs should be uncovered. You will be working from the ankles to the top of the thighs and there is no point having clothes in the way.

You cannot massage through clothes and since you will use oil you want to avoid getting it on the person's clothes. It is better if underwear is removed as well but unless you are massaging your spouse or partner this may prove embarrassing.

Position

Ask the person you massage to lie face downwards. It does not matter what position the head and arms are in except that they should be comfortable and the legs relaxed.

Some people find lying with their toes pointed uncomfortable. If this is the case put a pillow under the person's ankles or get him or her to move down the table or bench so that the feet are over the edge. Make sure there is some padding over the edge of the table or it will dig into the ankle.

It is better if the person does not watch what you are doing. There is a natural tendency to try to help which usually results in the area where you are working being tightened up.

Touch exercise

You will give a better massage if you understand the anatomy of the leg and its muscles. It also makes it more interesting. To develop some feel for what is where, start with an exercise in touch. Explore one leg first and then the other.

Back of the leg

Stand at the person's side (it does not matter which side) so that you are level with the feet. Compare the leg with Drawing 42 opposite. It shows the back of the calf and the thigh, first as you see them and then revealing some of

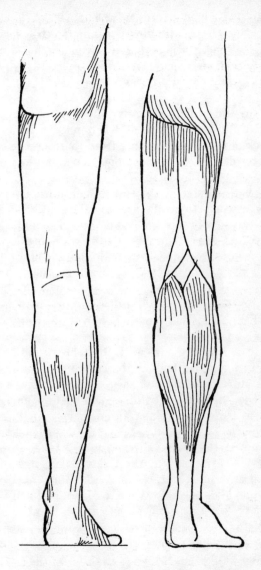

42 Back view of calf and thigh

the muscles which lie under the skin. See how many things shown in the drawing you can detect by looking at the person's leg. If the person has well developed muscles you may be able to see a lot but if he or she is fleshy or not very fit it may not be so easy.

Put your index finger, preferably of your right hand if you are right handed or left if left handed, on the knob at the back of the heel. Running from there up the calf is a tight, hard, but movable ridge. This is the archilles tendon.

Follow this ridge with your finger until it seems to disappear where the calf starts to enlarge. This is about a third of the way up the lower leg. The enlargement increases as you go further up the calf until it reduces shortly before the knee. This is the muscle of the back of the calf and one of the areas you will massage.

Hold the toes with one hand so that the person cannot point them. Then ask him or her to try to point the toes against your resistance. It is not necessary to push too strongly. A firm pressure is all that is required. While he or she is doing this look at the calf and you will see the muscle start to stand out as it contracts. If the person bends the knee before pointing the toes the muscle will stand out more. Do not ask him or her to push for long.

Have a short rest and then repeat This time while the muscle is contracted put the index finger of your other hand on the middle of it. Use a small amount of oil on your finger and slide it sideways across the leg until you feel the edge of the muscle. Run your finger along this edge.

Feel the edge of the muscle on both the inside and outside of the calf. You may have to get the person to relax and tighten up several times. If his or her muscular development is good this exercise is fairly easy.

Now repeat the exercise finding the edge of the muscle without the muscle being contracted.

Put your index finger on the outside knob of one of the ankles Move your finger up the middle of the outside of the leg from this knob and you will feel hard bone under your finger at first. See if you can follow the bone up the leg. This is easier to do on skinny people than on muscular or fleshy people. A little way below the knee you will come to a bump. This is the top end of the bone. There are two bones in the calf. You are following the outer and smaller one, the fibula.

Stand level with the knee At both the inside and outside edges of the crease at the back of the knee there is a tight, hard, moveable ridge, though thinner than the achilles tendon was. These are the hamstrings, the tendons connecting the calf bones to the muscles that run up the back of the thigh.

Using firm pressure with your index finger follow the muscles one at a time. Starting at the edges of the knee they gradually converge on the centre of the thigh, eventually joining onto a knob of bone just above the start of the buttocks.

To make the muscles stand out more put one hand on the person's heel and ask him or her to try to bend the knee so that the heel comes towards the buttocks. You should allow the heel to rise a foot off the surface and then resist any further movement. As with the calf muscles it should not be a contest of force but just firm pressure.

While the person is pushing against your hand use your other hand to follow the muscles. You may have to repeat this several times with rests inbetween. Then try to follow the muscles again without the person pushing.

Put your fingers on the outside of the person's thigh
just below the start of the buttocks. Using firm pressure,
move your hand upwards keeping your fingers in the
middle of the outside of the thigh. When your hand is
approximately level with the highest point of the buttocks
you will feel a bony knob under your fingers. This is the
outside of the hip joint.

Front of the leg

Ask the person to turn onto his or her back. Put a pillow
under the head. The hands can rest by the side or on the
stomach. Look at Drawing 43 opposite and compare what
you see. Note how many things shown in the drawing you
can detect on the actual legs.

Stand level with the calf Put your index finger with a
little oil on it on the front of the leg about six inches above
the ankle. Explore across the front of the calf starting
from the inside. Initially you will feel a hard rounded area
leading to a sharp ridge on the front. This is the second
and bigger of the two calf bones, the tibia.

Moving your finger further across you will feel the
softer but firm texture of muscle. This continues until you
reach the middle of the outside of the calf. Here you can
feel the hardness of bone again. This is the smaller of the
two calf bones which you felt earlier when the person was
lying on his or her front.

Explore these muscles and bones up to the knee by
running your finger along them and following their
course.

Move to the person's knee Gently but firmly hold the
knee cap. If the person has relaxed his or her thigh
muscles you will be able to move it round a little. Ask the
person to tighten the muscles on the front of the leg above

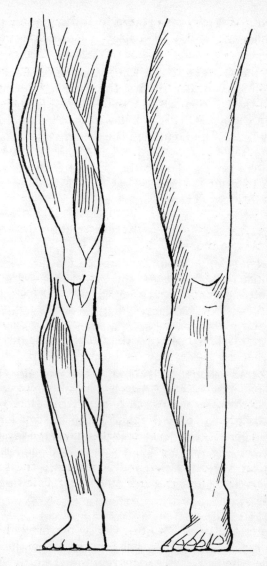

43 Front view of calf and thigh

the knee. You will see the knee cap tighten and move up a little. When the muscles are relaxed the opposite occurs.

Move your fingers off the knee cap and up the front of the thigh a few inches. At first there is a band about the width of the knee cap which is the tendon at the bottom of the thigh muscles. This is followed by the start of the thigh muscles. These muscles, the quadriceps or quads as they are called, cover the front of the thigh from just above the knee right up to the groin. Ask the person to tighten them and compare Drawing 43 on the previous page with what you see.

Relaxing the feet

Feet get terribly abused. They are designed for walking barefooted on soft uneven surfaces. However, we put them into shoes, often very tight ones with a variety of heels, and walk on hard unyielding pavements and floors. One result is feet get very tired, often aching a lot. You can do quite a lot to ease this by following the instructions below.

The person should be lying on his or her back. Put a pillow under the head if necessary.

Hold the big toe of one foot between the big knuckle and the smaller one above it with your index finger and thumb. With your other hand hold the toe between the nail and the smaller knuckle so that your hands are holding either side of the smaller knuckle.

Gently, without gripping too hard or being too vigorous, move the toe up and down with the second hand while keeping the first one still. You are thus alternately bending and straightening this knuckle. See Drawing 44 opposite.

Then move both your hands so that they are holding

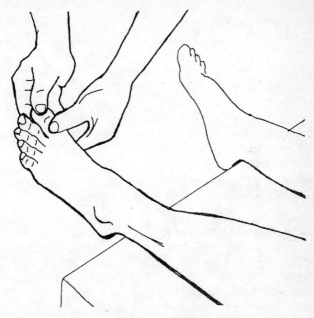

44 Relaxing the toes (1)

either side of the big knuckle, and repeat. Continue doing this for the other toes of both feet. Remember that the smaller toes have three knuckles and not two like the big toe. Deal with each knuckle separately.

Hold the big knuckle on the big toe between the index finger and thumb of one hand and hold the next toe similarly with the other hand. Move one hand up while moving the other hand down in a scissor movement, then repeat the other way round. Do not be too strong or you may hurt. Repeat this with the other toes. See Drawing 45 overleaf.

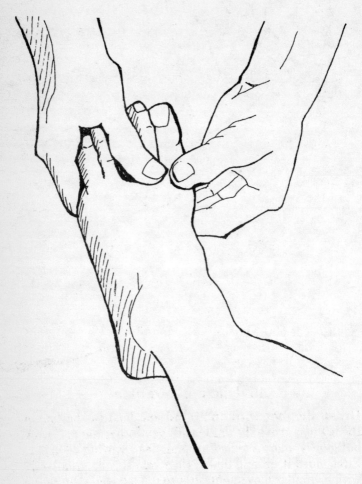

45 Relaxing the toes (2)

46 Relaxing the ankle

Grasp the foot with one hand and hold the bottom of
the leg just above the ankle with your other hand. Firmly
but gently, move the foot around. See Drawing 46 above.
First move it up and down, then side to side, and lastly
with a circular movement, first to the left and then to the
right. Make quite wide movements but don't be too
enthusiastic. If there is the slightest pain or discomfort
stop.

The other foot Repeat the above three exercises on the other foot. Chapter 13 discusses reflexology, a special type of foot massage.

Stroking the calf

The person you massage should lie on his or her front with legs slightly apart, as described on page 158.

Stand at the side of the person (it does not matter which side) so that you are just below the feet. You should be half facing towards the head with your outer foot pointing towards the head.

Put both hands above the ankle near you so that your thumbs meet in the middle. Using a small amount of oil on your hands, firmly but gently slide them up towards the knee. Apply pressure with your palms, not your fingers (see Drawing 47 opposite). The pressure should come from leaning your body weight onto your palms and not by pushing with your arms. Your fingers should rest on the flesh rather than do any work.

The distance you cover towards the knee depends on how tall you are and how long the person's legs are. If you find you start to overstretch you have gone far enough. Return to where you started keeping light skin contact.

With successive strokes move your hands further apart from each other by half an inch so that in a few strokes your hands are either side of the calf. Make sure that each stroke overlaps the previous one. Return to the start position keeping light skin contact.

Repeat with greater pressure. Continue this cycle gradually increasing the pressure each time until either you or the person feel that you are applying enough pressure. Unless the person has very muscular calves you should not apply a lot of pressure here.

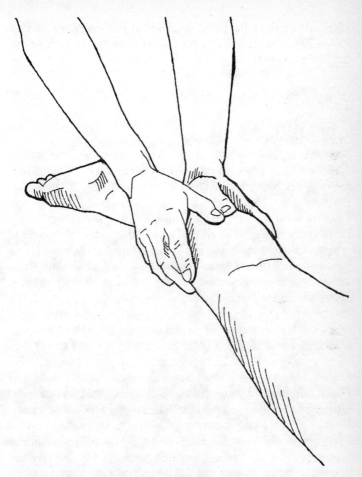

47 Stroking the calf

Then reduce the pressure gradually on each cycle until you are back where you started.

If you have not reached the knee move towards it and repeat. Stand a little below the new area and make sure that the strokes on the new area overlap the previous area.

If you plan to massage both legs repeat the above on the other calf. Go round to the other side or ask the person to turn round so that the head is where the feet were.

Kneading the calf

The person you massage should lie face downwards with the legs a few inches apart. He or she should lie as near to you as possible without feeling insecure if on a table or bench.

Stand close facing the calf muscles. The closer you are, the better.

Knead the far sides of both calves from this position. To knead the near sides go round to the other side or ask the person you are massaging to turn round so that the head is where the feet were.

Use one hand, preferably your strong one (right if you are right handed, left if you are left handed). Rest your other hand on the leg.

Place the heel of your hand with a little oil on it on the centre of the nearer calf just where the achilles tendon disappears and the muscles starts to enlarge. Let your fingers rest on the calf.

Keeping your finger tips where they are, move the heel of your hand towards them. Your hand will move away from you towards the far side of the calf and the flesh lying between the heel of your hand and the ends of your fingers will get squeezed. See Drawing 48.

The pressure in massage comes from using your body weight and here the pressure comes from applying your body weight through the heel of your hand. Your fingers

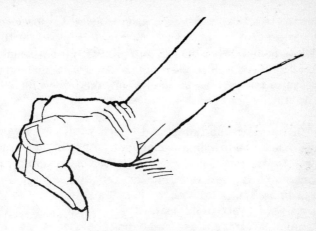

48 Kneading the calf

apply a resistance to this movement and thus the muscle gets kneaded between them.

Take care not to pull your fingers towards the heel of your hand. If you do you may pinch the calf and you will not be able to apply much pressure. Also ensure that your finger tips do not dig into the calf. It is not the actual tips which should be pressing on the calf but the pads at the end of your fingers.

When the heel of your hand has reached your finger ends keep it where it is and stretch out your fingers so that they rest further round the calf. Then repeat the kneading action moving the heel of your hand to your fingers. When you cannot go any futher round move your hand back to the middle of the calf, keeping light skin contact.

Move your hand about half a hand width further up the calf and do the same. Continue until you reach the top of the calf, just below the knees.

Return to where you started keeping light skin contact and repeat with greater pressure. Continue to do this, each time increasing the pressure, until eventually you or the person you are massaging feel there is enough pressure. Then gradually reduce the pressure as you built it up until you get back to the initial level.

Both hands Swap hands and knead with your weaker one. When you are happy using your other hand you are ready to use both together. The method of kneading with each hand is the same but they should be used in a co-ordinated manner with your hands alternating.

Start with your hand nearer the person's head. As it is finishing its stroke the second hand should come in nearer the foot but slightly overlapping the first one. Then as that hand is finishing its stroke the first hand should restart nearer the head and again slightly overlapping the previous stroke.

It helps if you turn the currently working hand onto its little finger side as it finishes its stroke. This gives space for the next hand to start without any loss of contact between strokes.

If you are only massaging this one leg, go round to the other side or ask the person to turn round so that the head is where the feet were. Then repeat the above on the other side of the calf.

If you are massaging both legs knead the far side of the other calf and then do the other side of both legs as described above.

Massage the calf from the front

Another way to massage the calf is for the person to lie on his or her back. The knee should be bent and the foot resting on the surface. Use one hand to steady the knee. To prevent the person's foot sliding, rest one of your

knees, or else sit, on the surface in front of the foot.
Drawing 49 below illustrates the position.

The massage to use in this position is kneading with one
hand as described above. Instead of working from the
middle of the calf out to the side, work from the outside to
the middle. Then change hands and work from the other
outside back to the middle.

The advantage of this position is that the calf muscle
hangs loose so it is easy to feel and massage. It may also

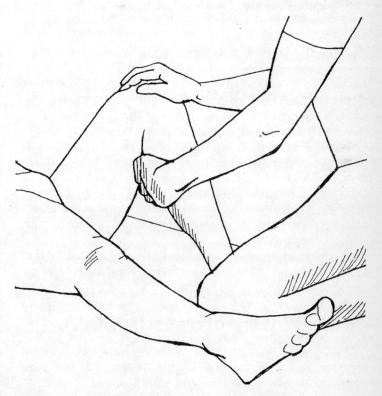

49 Position to massage calf

be more comfortable for the person to lie on his or her
back. However there are disadvantages. You have to
ensure that the person's foot does not slip, you have to use
one hand to support the knee, and you cannot go straight
from massaging the calf to massaging the back of the
thigh. Nevertheless, if you only want to massage the calf
this is a good way.

Stroking the back of the thigh

The person you massage should lie on his or her front.
Make sure he or she is near the side of the bench or table
and that you are standing close. Stand just below the
knee, half facing towards the head with your outer foot
pointing towards the head.

Start just above the knee Put both hands above the
back of the knee near you so that your thumbs meet in the
middle. Using a small amount of oil on your hands firmly
but gently slide them up the thigh. Pressure should be
applied using your palms, not the fingers. Your fingers
should rest on the flesh rather than do any work. Drawing
47 on page 169 shows the technique being applied to the
calf. The pressure should be applied by leaning your body
weight onto your palms and not by pushing with your
arms.

The distance that you cover depends on how tall you are
and how long the person's legs are. If you start to
overstretch you have gone far enough.

With successive strokes move your hands further apart
from each other by about half an inch so that each stroke
overlaps the previous one. When you reach the sides of the
thigh return to the start position keeping light skin
contact.

Make sure that as your hands get further apart with

successive strokes you massage the inside and outside of the thighs. Do not just massage the back and ignore the sides. It is very easy to make this mistake but the muscles on the sides of the thighs also benefit from massage.

Repeat with greater pressure Continue this cycle each time increasing the pressure until you or the person feel there is enough pressure. You can apply much more pressure here than you did on the calf.

Then reduce the pressure gradually as you built it up until you are back where you started.

The thigh should be massaged right up to the buttocks. If you have not reached them, move towards them and repeat. Make sure that you overlap the previous area.

Kneading the back of the thigh

There are two methods for kneading this area. The first is how you kneaded the calf with the person lying on his or her front. Start just above the knee and continue right up to the buttocks.

The second method is especially useful if the person has a very big build and you have small hands. The person's and your position are the same, but here you will knead the muscle not between the heel of your hand and your fingers but between the heel of your hand and the thigh bone deep inside those muscles.

Put the heel of your hand, preferably your stronger hand, on the middle of the back of the person's thigh just above the knee. Let your fingers rest on the skin as they do not play any part in the massage.

With your elbow slightly bent lean gently onto the heel of your hand so that it starts to press into the flesh. Maintaining that lean and pressure, slide your hand slowly away from you towards the far side of the thigh.

Your fingers should slide on the surface and not resist the movement. Remember to use a little oil.

Keep this movement up until your hand has reached the side of the thigh and is about to slip off it. See Drawing 50 below.

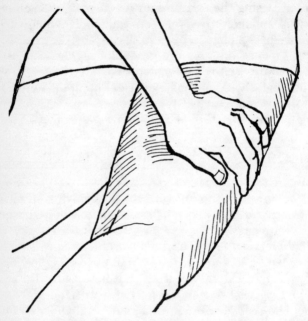

50 Kneading the back of thigh

Return to where you started maintaining light skin contact. Move up the thigh by half a hand width and do it again. Carry on moving up the thigh until you start to bend over to the side. Return to the start position above the knee.

Repeat with greater pressure Continue doing this

increasing the pressure each time until either of you feels that there is enough pressure. Then gradually reduce the pressure in the same way as you built it up.

Extra pressure If you need to use extra pressure you can do so by placing the heel of your free hand on the back of your massaging hand. Then apply pressure by leaning through both hands. Drawing 51 below shows the position of the hands.

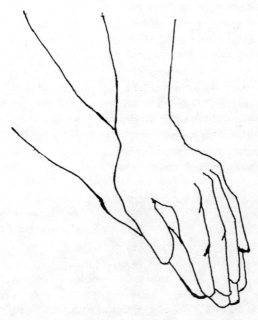

51 Hand to reinforce kneading

When you have finished this area move your feet so that you are further up the thigh and repeat, starting slightly below where you left off. You should knead the far side of both thighs, from just above the knees right up to the buttocks.

To massage the nearer sides go round to the other side of the person or get the person to turn round so that the head is where the feet were.

Both hands Swap hands so that you use your weaker hand. When you are happy using it you can start using both hands together. Of course you cannot do this if you are reinforcing one hand with the other.

Use both hands alternately, not simultaneously. The method of kneading with each hand is the same but they should be used in a co-ordinated manner with the hands alternating.

Start off with your hand which is nearer the person's head. As it is finishing its stroke the second hand should come in, nearer the foot but slightly overlapping the first one. Then as that hand is finishing its stroke the first hand should restart, nearer the head and again slightly overlapping the previous stroke.

It helps if you turn the currently working hand onto its little finger side as it finishes its stroke. This gives space for the next hand to start without any loss of contact between strokes.

Massage the front of the thighs

The person you are massaging should lie on his or her back. Put a pillow under the head. The hands can rest by the side or on the stomach. Make sure he or she is close to the side of the table and close to you.

Stroke the front of the thigh in the same way that you stroked the back of the thigh. Start just above the knee. Go towards the pelvis stopping before the groin. Your hands should start together in the middle of the thigh and work outwards with successive strokes. Continue until they reach the inner and outer sides of the thigh.

Return to where you started keeping light skin contact and repeat with greater pressure. Continue to do this, each time increasing the pressure, until eventually you or the person feel there is enough pressure. Then gradually reduce the pressure as you built it up until you get back to the initial level.

Next knead the front of the thigh, using either method described for kneading the back of the thigh.

Order of massage

If you only want to massage one area use the stroking technique first and then the kneading technique. However, if you intend to massage both legs, start with stroking the back of the calf and thigh of one leg and then the other.

Next knead the sides of the legs away from you, first the calf and thigh of one leg then the other. Then move to the other side and knead the other sides.

Then ask the person to turn onto his or her back and similarly massage the front of the thighs, starting off with stroking both legs and then kneading them first on the sides away from you and then going round to knead the other sides.

12
Arm massage

People get aches and pain in their arms from time to time throughout their lives. For the most part the discomfort results from overuse or misuse. Typical symptoms include tightness and aches which are more common in the forearm and shoulders than the upper arm. Often there may be pain after a particular activity or sport. While this may simply be due to a slight strain it should be properly diagnosed by a doctor, qualified osteopath or physiotherapist. Similarly if pins and needles or a burning sensation are complained of get a diagnosis since these symptoms often stem from trouble in the spine.

Tennis and golfer's elbow

Two common complaints are tennis elbow and its opposite number golfer's elbow. Both are strains of the muscles and tendons in the forearm where they attach to the bone on either side of the elbow. Tennis elbow refers to the outside of the elbow and golfer's elbow to the inside of the elbow. Massage can help these although they may be too severe for relief by massage alone. Other treatment may include acupuncture and physiotherapy. A doctor may use a cortisone injection and surgery can be involved if the injury is very bad.

Clothing

The arm should be bare up to and including the shoulder. In practice this means a shirt or blouse and vest should be taken off. If you are massaging a woman ask her to slip her bra strap off her shoulder and arm. If she feels embarrassed or uneasy she can cover her bust with a towel.

There is no point in massaging through clothing, it does not work. If you remove too little clothes you will get oil on them. You will also feel cramped if any clothes get in the way.

Position

The person you massage should lie on his or her back. The hands should rest by the sides or on the abdomen. Put a pillow under the head although a few people are happier without one. If the surface is hard you may need to put a pillow or cushion under the small of the back. The person must be comfortable in order to relax.

An elderly person may feel happier sitting rather than lying down. Make sure he or she is comfortable. In particular ensure that the low part of the back is well supported with pillows. The hands should be by the side or resting on the person's lap. While you massage, the person should be able to relax, lean back and let you get on with it. If he or she has to sit unsupported or in an uncomfortable position you will be wasting your time.

Touch exercise on the forearm

Stand at the person's side (it does not matter which side) so that you are level with his or her hand. Look at the hand and arm. Compare them with Drawings 52 and 53 on pages 182 and 183. The drawings show the arm as you

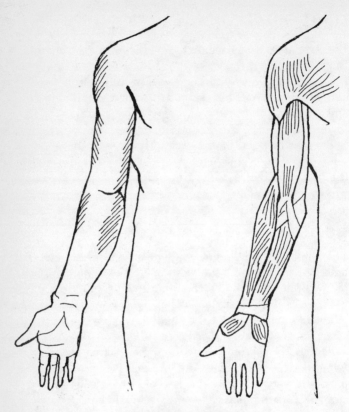

52 Front of arm

see it, viewed from the front and the back, and with some
of the muscles which lie under the skin. See if you can get
a sense of how the muscles flow under the skin.

Hold the person's hand in your hand With the index
finger of your other hand explore each finger and the
thumb from the finger nails to the knuckles. Use a little
oil on your finger.

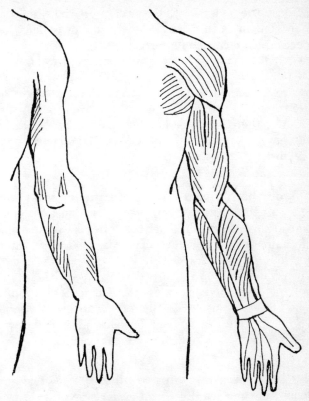

53 Back of arm

There is a bone about an inch and a half long running from each knuckle towards the wrist. With your finger follow the bone from the index finger knuckle until you cannot follow it any further. Return your finger to just before the knuckle and slide your finger sideways off this bone. You will find a groove and then the bone from the next knuckle. Follow this bone. Repeat for all the fingers and the thumb.

Move to the wrist Just above the wrist you can feel two knobs, one on each side. These are the lower ends of the bones which form the forearm.

With the person's arm turned palm upwards the two forearm bones lie side by side. Try to follow each bone towards the elbow using your index finger. If the person is thin you may be able to identify these two bones by touch. However there is often a lot of muscle in the way and you may have to press very hard. Give up if you need to press too hard.

Put your hand two inches below the person's elbow with your thumb and fingers on opposite sides of the arm. Then ask the person to clench his or her fist very strongly. The palm should still face upwards. Feel the tightened muscles.

Look at the arm and see if you can see the muscles tighten. You may also see the tendons which connect some of these muscles to the wrist and fingers tighten. Although there are tendons on both sides of the wrists they are more visible on the palm side.

The main muscle groups in the forearm start at the elbow from the two knobs on either side of it. Put your hand just below the knob on the inner side of the elbow. With your thumb on the front of the arm and your index finger on the back you can feel the muscle between them. Follow the bulge of these muscles down the forearm. Near the wrist the bulge seems to get less and you can start to feel the bone.

If the person is not muscular you may feel the bone all the way up the forearm, while if he or she is very muscular you may not feel it until you are very near the wrist.

Repeat this on the outer side of the arm. If you are not

sure if you are feeling the muscle ask the person to clench the fist again and you will feel it stand out.

Upper arm

On either side of the elbow are the two knobs that you felt before. These are at the bottom of the upper arm bone, the humerus, which runs from the elbow to the shoulder.

With the palm face up ask the person to bend the arm so that the forearm is lifted up about six inches. Run your index finger across the crease at the elbow. You can feel, and may be able to see, a tight line crossing the crease from above to below it. This is the tendon of the biceps muscle. The muscle runs down the front of the upper arm from the shoulder to the elbow.

Hold the person's hand and ask him or her to try to bend the arm while you resist. This makes the muscle and tendon stand out more. Look at them and then explore them with your other hand.

Repeat with the arm relaxed, first bent while you hold his or her hand, and then out straight. Notice how the bulge of muscle rapidly disappears as you reach either side of the arm. Also notice that the bulk of the muscle only occupies the middle third or so of the upper arm.

Examine the back of the arm Lift the person's arm up with one hand and feel the back of the arm with the other. With the elbow bent ask him or her to try to straighten the arm gently while you resist. Feel the muscle at the back of the arm bulging. This is called the triceps.

Ask the person to relax and see if you can still feel it. It is less obvious than the one in the front of the arm and harder to find when relaxed.

Move to the outside of the arm About two thirds of the

way up the outside of the arm you will notice a bulge starting. As it nears the shoulder it widens until it ends on the shoulder. This is the deltoid muscle.

Ask the person to move the arm sideways away from the body. When the elbow is about six inches from the side use one of your hands to prevent any further movement by restraining the elbow. The person should carry on trying to move the arm against your resistance. With your other hand feel the muscle and note how it has hardened. Ask the person to relax and notice the difference.

Compare what you have felt and found with Drawings 52 and 53 on pages 182 and 183. The better your sense of what is where the better your massage will be.

Relaxing the hands

Lightly hold the person's index finger between the nail and end knuckle with your index finger and thumb. The palm should face downwards. With your other hand hold the same finger between the end knuckle and next knuckle so that you are gripping either side of the end knuckle. Gently move your first hand up and down while keeping the second one still. You are thus alternately bending and straightening the end knuckle. Do not be too strong or enthusiastic. Move your hands so you hold either side of the next knuckle and repeat, (see Drawing 54 below). Then do the same with the big knuckle. Do this with all four fingers and thumb of both hands.

54 Relaxing the fingers (1)

Hold his or her middle finger at the big knuckle
where the finger joins the hand with your thumb and
index finger. Similarly hold the person's index finger with
your other hand. See Drawing 55 below. Gently, firmly
and slowly move the person's middle finger upwards and
the index finger downwards by a small amount in a
scissors movement. Then reverse the direction. Repeat
several times so that you are moving the two fingers up
and down in opposite directions to each other. Do not grip
too tightly and do not move them too far or you will hurt
and may cause injury. Repeat this between the other
fingers of both hands.

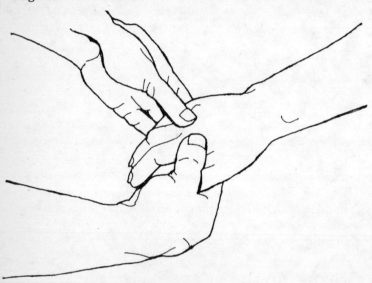

55 Relaxing the fingers (2)

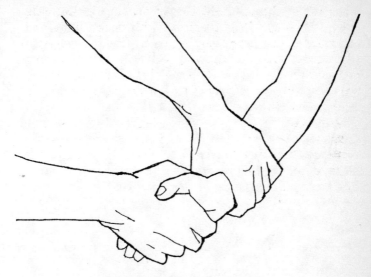

56 Relaxing the wrist

Hold the person's hand as for a handshake Holding
the wrist still with your other hand, move his or her hand
backwards, forwards, sideways and then around. See
Drawing 56 above. Don't be too strong and never force the
hand or take it further than is comfortable. Encourage the
person to relax. If he or she cannot, make sure you are not
gripping too hard or being too energetic.

Stroking the forearm

The person you massage should lie on his or her back with
arms by the side. If this is awkward, the person can sit but
make sure he or she is comfortable. In particular ensure
the low part of the back is well supported with pillows.

   Stand by the side of the arm you want to massage,
facing towards the head.

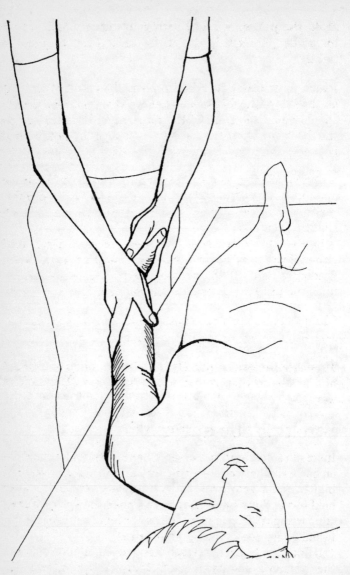

57 Stroking the forearm

Hold the person's hand with your nearer hand so that his or her forearm is raised. Be careful not to grip too tightly.

Place your other hand with a small amount of oil on it on the side of the forearm just above the wrist. The thumb should be on the front of the forearm and the fingers on the back so that the side of the arm is sandwiched between them. See Drawing 57 opposite.

Exerting gentle even pressure with both your thumb and index finger slide your hand up the forearm until you reach the elbow. Return to the wrist and repeat with slightly greater pressure.

Repeat this increasing the pressure each time until either of you feels you are exerting enough pressure. Then gradually ease off the pressure with successive strokes until the pressure is back to the starting level.

Change your hands so that you are massaging the other side of his or her arm with your other hand.

Massage the other arm Go round to the other side or get him or her to turn round so the head is where the feet were.

Stroking the upper arm

Instead of holding the person's hand with yours, hold his or her wrist between your nearer arm and your side. The higher under your arm the wrist is placed the better your hold on it. Your hand should be under the person's arm, supporting it. This leaves your outer hand completely free to massage. See Drawing 58 overleaf.

If your arms are short, so that you are unable to reach the person's shoulder comfortably, move nearer the shoulder. In this case grip the forearm, rather than the

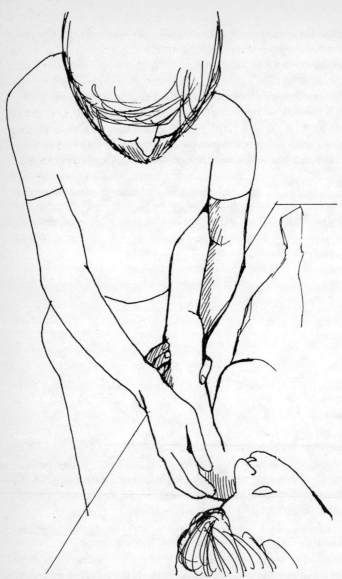

58 Stroking the upper arm

wrist, between your arm and side. It is important that the wrist or forearm is held in some way. Unlike the legs, trunk or neck, the arm has a large range of movement and should be restrained when you massage it. Otherwise the person will tense muscles to keep the arm still.

If his or her arms are much shorter than yours, you will not need to do this. Hold his or her hand with your nearer hand and use your other hand to massage the arm.

It does not matter which side you stand but initially hold the person's wrist or forearm using your arm nearer to him or her, so that your outer arm is free to massage.

Place the palm of your free hand with a little oil on it on the front of the arm just above the elbow. Your thumb and fingers should rest on the skin.

Slide your hand up the arm and over the shoulder gently but firmly. Apply pressure with your palm, not the fingers. Return to the starting position using light skin contact.

The next stroke starts a little to the outside of the arm, slightly overlapping the previous stroke. With successive strokes work round the arm covering the outside and then the back.

Return to the start maintaining light skin contact and repeat with greater pressure. Continue this cycle increasing the pressure each time until either of you feels there is enough. Then reduce it gradually over successive strokes until you return to the starting pressure.

Change hands so that your inner hand is free to massage. Start off with the front again, but this time cover the inside and then the back in the same way as you did the outside.

Kneading the forearm

Return to the forearm. The person you massage should lie on his or her back with arms by the side. This is the best position but if it is awkward, the person can sit.

Stand by the side of the arm you want to massage, facing towards the head.

Hold the person's hand with your hand nearer him or her. Be careful not to grip too tightly.

Place your other hand, with a small amount of oil on the thumb, on the side of the forearm just above the wrist. The thumb should be on the front of the forearm and the fingers on the back so that the side of the arm is sandwiched between them. See Drawing 57 on page 190.

Slide your thumb towards your fingers Your fingers should stay where they are while your thumb moves towards them so that the flesh gets kneaded between your thumb and fingers. Be careful not to pinch or dig your thumb or fingers in. The kneading action takes place between the pads of the thumb and fingers and not between their tips. See Drawing 59 opposite.

Move your hand up the person's arm by half an inch keeping light skin contact and repeat. When you have reached the elbow return to the wrist keeping light skin contact.

Repeat with greater pressure Each time you return to the wrist gradually increase the pressure. Continue in this fashion until you or the person you are massaging feel you are applying enough pressure.

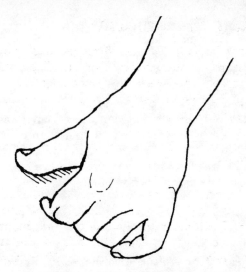

59 Thumb kneading the arm

Gradually reduce the pressure as you built it up until you are back at the starting pressure.

Change hands and knead the other side of the forearm.

Kneading the upper arm

To knead the upper arm adopt the same position as for stroking the upper arm. Hold the person's wrist between your arm and your side. The higher under your arm the wrist is placed the better your hold on it. Your hand of that arm should be under the person's arm supporting it. This leaves one hand completely free to massage. See Drawing 58 on page 192.

If your arms are short, so that you are unable to reach the person's shoulder comfortably, move nearer the shoulder. Grip the forearm, rather than the wrist, between your arm and side.

If the person's arms are much shorter than yours hold his or her hand with one of your hands and use your other hand to massage.

Start with the front of the arm Place your hand just above the crease of the elbow so that your thumb is on the inside of the arm and the fingers on the outside. Now slide your thumb towards your fingers. See Drawing 59 on the previous page. Be careful not to pinch.

Successive strokes should be half an inch above the previous ones and continue until you stretch too far or have reached the shoulder. When you have kneaded as far as you can return to the start keeping skin contact.

Repeat with greater pressure Each time you return to the start, gradually increase the pressure. Eventually one of you will feel that you are applying enough pressure.

Reduce the pressure gradually as you built it up until you have returned to the starting position.

If you have not reached the shoulder, move nearer to it adjusting your hold on the person's arm. Repeat the massage on the new area. Make sure that you overlap the previous area by a little.

Knead the outside of the upper arm

Hold the person's arm with your inner hand with the wrist or forearm between your arm and side so that your outer hand is free to knead the outside of the arm. See Drawing 58 on page 192.

Remember from the touch exercise that the muscle on

the outside of the arm starts about two thirds of the way
up the upper part of the arm.

Place the palm of your hand just below the start of the
outside upper arm muscle so that your thumb and
forefinger rest either side of it.

Slide your thumb with some oil on it towards your
fingers in the same way you did when kneading the front
of the arm. See Drawing 59 on page 195. Be careful not to
pinch and do not move your fingers.

If you are unable to knead the full width of the muscle
in one stroke do several strokes. When your thumb has
reached your fingers it should stay where it is. Stretch out
your fingers and let them rest on the skin further round
the arm. Then knead the thumb towards the fingers in
their new position.

If necessary repeat this several times until you have
covered the muscle.

Move your hand up half an inch keeping light skin
contact and repeat. When you have kneaded as far as you
can reach return to the start.

Repeat with greater pressure Each time you return to
the start, gradually increase the pressure. Eventually one
of you will feel that you are applying enough pressure.

Reduce the pressure gradually as you built it up until
you have returned to the starting pressure.

If you have not reached the shoulder, move nearer to
it adjusting your hold on the person's arm. Repeat the
massage on the new area. Make sure that you overlap the
previous area by a little.

Large upper arm muscles

If the person has very big upper arm muscles there is another method of kneading. Stand facing the upper arm. The person's arm should rest on the surface if he or she is lying down. Hold the forearm with your nearer hand to stop it moving about. If the person is seated, support the forearm with your nearer hand.

Place the heel of your other hand on top of the upper arm just above the elbow, with the fingers resting on the inside of the arm and some oil on your hand. Keeping your fingers where they are, move the heel of your hand slowly towards them, kneading the flesh between the heel of your hand and your fingers. See Drawing 60 below. Your fingers should not dig into the skin and they should not slide over it. The heel of your hand does the sliding. See page 89 if you are unsure where the heel of your hand is.

If you have very small hands and the person has very large muscles you may have to do a second stroke to reach

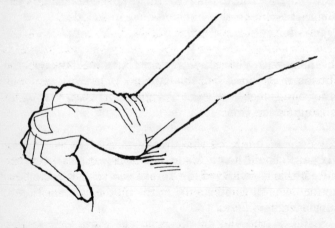

60 Kneading the upper arm

sufficiently far round the side. In this case when the heel of your hand has reached your fingers the heel should stay where it is. Stretch out your fingers and let them rest on the skin further round the arm. Then move the heel of the hand towards the fingers in their new position. If necessary repeat this two or three times.

The next stroke should start about half a hand width further up the arm. Repeat the stroke described above. When you have reached the shoulder return to just above the elbow and repeat the cycle with greater pressure. Continue repeating the cycle, increasing the pressure each time. Eventually one of you will feel that you are applying enough pressure.

Reduce the pressure gradually as you built it up until you have returned to the starting pressure.

Kneading towards the outside of the arm with this method may be more awkward because you have to twist round to get your hand correctly positioned with your fingers resting on the outside of the arm.

An alternative position is for the person to stretch the arm out at right angles to the trunk while you stand on the inside of it. Your fingers will naturally fall towards the outside of the arm. You must support the arm with your other hand since it will not be supported unless the person is lying on the floor.

Knead the back of the upper arm The person you massage should lie on his or her back with arms by the side. If this is awkward the person can sit but make sure he or she is comfortable with the lower back well supported by pillows.

Stand by the side of the arm you want to massage, facing towards the head.

Hold the person's wrist or forearm between your arm and your side. Your hand should be under the person's arm supporting it. This leaves your other hand completely free to massage. See Drawing 58 on page 192. Use either hand here. Make sure your grip is not too hard or too slack as the person will tense up.

Place your hand on the back of the arm just above the elbow, using a small amount of oil. The thumb should be on one side of the muscle and the fingers on the other. Move your thumb towards the index finger without your index finger moving. Use the front pads of your finger and thumb and not the tips.

If the person's arm is broad you may have to do several strokes before you have kneaded the full width of the muscle. When your thumb has reached your index finger, it should stay put while the fingers stretch out again. Then the thumb again kneads towards the index finger. When you have kneaded the width of the muscle return to where you started keeping light skin contact.

Move up half an inch keeping light skin contact and repeat. Carry on until you have reached the back of the shoulder. Then return to the start keeping light skin contact and repeat, applying more pressure. Repeat this cycle, increasing the pressure each time until there is enough. Then gradually reduce it as you built it up until you have reached the starting pressure.

Massage the other arm

After you have finished massaging one arm, massage the other. Go round to the other side of the person, or ask him or her to turn round so that the feet are where the head was. Then repeat. Stroke the forearm and upper arm first. Then knead both parts of the arm.

13
Foot massage –
reflexology

Reflexology is a method of massaging the feet to improve your general health. It is easy to learn and use. It originated long before modern medicine was developed when people discovered that by massaging the feet, and especially specific areas of them, they could help problems that had no apparent relationship to the feet. By a process of trial and error these areas became more and more defined until their positions were clearly located.

Reflexologists believe that a large range of disorders can be helped ranging from aching joints to problems with specific organs. Reflexology can also help your body function better as a whole. By working on all the areas of the foot you can generally improve the health of a person. However, this improvement will not come about from one session of reflexology. Improving health is a process that takes time and regular sessions are needed to produce results.

This chapter describes how to massage the reflex areas on the sole of the foot and introduces you to the basic skills of reflexology. Like all skills your performance will improve with practice and experience.

There are also reflex areas on the top of the foot, the bottom of the calf just above the heel and on the hands. These are not described here. Nevertheless with this chapter you can give a competent general reflexology massage. If you wish to know more about reflexology and the other reflex areas refer to the books mentioned in the list of useful reading on page 238.

When not to use reflexology

● Do not work over wounds, sores or scars.
● Do not work directly on varicose veins, ulcers, corns or callouses.
● Do not massage the bones and tendons in the feet. Pressing directly on them can be painful.
● Do not massage a pregnant woman.
● Do not massage a woman if she is having her period.
● Avoid massage after an operation, or if a person is unwell or recovering from an illness. Consult a doctor first for an accurate diagnosis.
● If the person you are going to massage has eaten a big meal, wait for an hour until it has been partly digested.
● Remember that children are more sensitive than adults and can react more quickly and strongly. Use less strength and work for a shorter time, especially if the child is very young. Similarly be gentle with the elderly.
● What you are doing can affect the whole body. If the person is ill do not take risks.

Position

Sitting The person being massaged should sit in a comfortable chair with his or her feet stretched out and resting on a coffee table or low chair or stool. Put a cushion on the surface if it is hard. The feet should be high enough so that you can massage comfortably.

Lying The person should lie comfortably on his or her back. If the surface is hard, cover it with some blankets or a duvet and a sheet. Put a pillow under the head, and one under the knees or low back if necessary. If the person is not comfortable he or she will wriggle around and you will not be able to massage.

Your position You need to be sitting comfortably. If you are not you cannot concentrate on what you are doing. The best position is for you to sit on the floor or an upright chair or stool. The person's feet should be slightly below the level of your shoulders. Then you can hold the feet comfortably while at the same time see what you are doing.

Make sure that there are no draughts and if you are at home tell family and friends to deal with the telephone and not to interrupt you.

Reflex areas

Drawings 61 and 62 (on pages 204 and 205) show the soles of both feet. Each drawing depicts the reflex areas which relate to various parts of the body. Look at the numbered areas and work out which area corresponds to which part of the body. By working over each reflex area you can stimulate the functioning of that part of the body. Study these drawings so that you become familiar with the various reflex areas.

Technique

The technique of reflexology massage is very simple. You apply firm, sometimes strong, pressure with your thumb onto the various reflex areas shown in Drawings 61 and 62 on pages 204 and 205. You only use one hand to massage. The other hand supports the foot against the

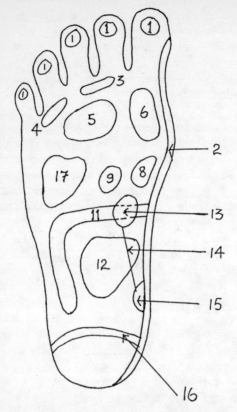

61 Reflex areas of right foot

Key to reflex areas on both feet

The following areas apply to both feet except for 7 and 10 which are only on the left foot and 17 which is only on the right foot.

1	Sinuses	3	Eyes
2	Spine	4	Ears

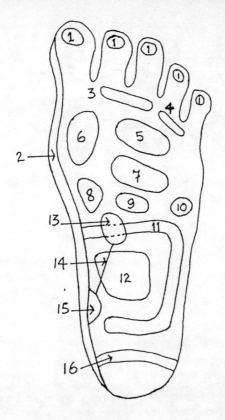

62 Reflex areas of left foot

  5 Lung
  6 Thyroid
  7 Heart
  8 Stomach
  9 Pancreas
 10 Spleen
 11 Large intestine

 12 Small intestine
 13 Kidneys
 14 Ureter
 15 Bladder
 16 Sciatic
 17 Liver

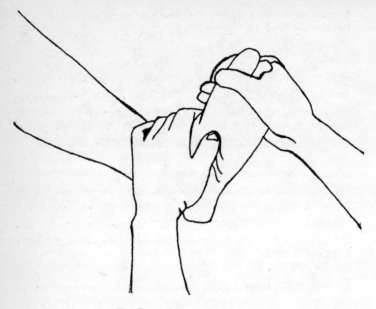

63 Reflexology technique

pressure your thumb exerts. Drawing 63 above illustrates the position.

It does not matter which hand you use but your right hand will be easiest to use if you are right handed, or your left hand if you are left handed.

Choose the area to work on Hold the foot with your working hand so that your thumb is on the area. Your other hand should be on the top surface of the foot on the other side of the area you massage.

Press your thumb into the area and at the same time move it in a very small circle either clockwise or anti-clockwise. Use as near to the tip of your thumb as you can without digging your nail in. Do not slide the thumb over the surface. It should only move by a fraction of an inch. You do not need any oil, talc or cream with this massage.

Maintain the pressure with your thumb for two or three seconds while doing slow circles. Then release your thumb and move it slightly. The new position should be immediately next to the previous one. The movement should be smooth and continuous, not jerky. With a little practice it is easy to do.

Repeat the pressure and circular movement It is important that the new position is immediately beside the old position so that you do not miss any of the reflex area.

Carry on massaging the area in this way until you have covered it all.

Direction of movement When massaging an area it does not matter whether you work over it from left to right, top to bottom or in a circular fashion. The important thing is that you work over as much of the area as possible.

Do not apply too much pressure Everyone has a different ability to tolerate pain. The degree of pressure which one person can handle may be too much for another.

Start with only light pressure and gradually increase it until you use as much as the person on the receiving end can comfortably take. As you gain confidence you will find you can judge how much to use.

However, if a particular point or area is more tender than the rest of the foot this is an indication that the area needs attention. Make a mental note of the area and when you have finished massaging the whole of the foot return to this area and work on it until the discomfort has cleared.

Start of massage

Before you start a reflexology massage you should relax the feet and ankles. This is described in detail on page 164.

Always give an overall reflexology massage of the feet first. When you have completed this you can go back to the areas which need special attention. Often the overall massage is sufficient. As well as helping the whole of the body, it may also help a particular problem as well.

The order of massage set out here is commonly used but if you feel another order is better by all means use it. What you must do is stick to a particular order. If your massage has a plan and consistency behind it the person on the recieving end will be able to relax and let you get on with it. If you are doing it in a piecemeal fashion the person will start to move around and become impatient.

In the description of the massage below, the inside of the foot refers to the big toe side, and the outside of the foot refers to the little toe side. All the massage is done on the sole of the foot.

Order of Massage

Start with the sole of the person's left foot, which is on your right. Drawing 62 on page 205 shows the reflex areas which are numbered to help you find them.

Sinuses The areas involving the sinuses are found on the pads at the ends of the toes. They go from the tips of the toes down to just before the first crease (1). Your massage should go in that direction.

Massage all the toes, starting with the big toe and ending with the little toe.

Spine This area runs down the inside (big toe) edge of the foot from the top of the big toe to the heel (2). Start at the top of this area and work down it until you reach the heel.

Eyes and ears Follow the second toe downwards from its tip to where it joins the rest of the foot. The areas for these two parts of the body run from here towards the little toe (3,4). Work from the inside towards the outside of the foot.

Lung and thyroid Below the eye area is the lung area, and then on the inside of the foot around the ball of the foot is the thyroid area (5,6). Massage these in the same way as before, working across the foot from the outside to the inside.

Heart Just to the outside of the bottom of the thyroid area is the heart area (7). This runs across the foot below the lung area. This area is only on the left foot. Work outwards over the area.

Digestive system On the inside of the foot below the thyroid area is the stomach area (8). Moving towards the outside from here is the pancreas area (9) and then near the outside of the foot is the spleen area (10). Work outwards over these.

Return to the inside of the foot. Below the stomach area are the intestines areas. As you can see from drawing 62 on page 205, there are separate areas for the large and small intestines. Work over the small intestine area first (12). Then work along the large intestine area (11) from where it starts on the inside of the foot just below the stomach area. Follow its course until it ends, again on the inside of the foot but this time below the small intestine area.

Kidneys and bladder The area for the kidney starts a little way from the inside of the foot along the large intestine area (13). The bladder area is on the inside of the foot just above the end of the large intestine area (15).

Start at the kidney area and then work downwards at an angle towards the bladder area. By doing so you cover the area of the ureter (14), the tube that connects these two organs together.

Sciatic area This runs across the sole of the foot just above the heel (16). It is used if the person is suffering from sciatica, and is not normally included in a general massage.

Massage the right foot

Having massaged the left foot repeat the procedure on the right foot. Drawing 61 on page 204 shows the reflex areas. The areas are very similar except that the right foot has the liver and gall bladder areas (17), and no heart or spleen area. The large intestine area (11) is a little different from that on the left foot. It starts near the outside of the foot and runs up parallel with the outside of the foot until it is above the small intestine area. It then runs towards the inside of the foot. It should be massaged in that order after you have completed the small intestine area (12).

14
Pregnancy

Pregnancy for most women and their men is a time of hope, happiness and joyful anticipation as they plan for the future with their new baby. But this period has its problems: backaches, swollen ankles and wrists, varicose veins, headaches and tiredness. They may be accepted as part of the normal process of being pregnant and that nothing can be done. But this is not true.

Massage can give considerable relief provided there is no medical problem which needs attention and your doctor has no objection. It is also a great way to improve communication between expectant parents. A time set aside to give comfort and relaxation helps both parties, the pregnant woman and her husband or boyfriend who is giving the massage. This is even more important if there are children around with their demands to be met.

Massage is not difficult and it is no more difficult because of pregnancy. The only problem is that the 'bump' in front can make sitting and lying awkward.

This chapter shows how to use massage to help the discomforts arising in pregnancy and describes the positions to use. Also read Chapter 7 on page 78 which gives general tips on how to massage. For a more general massage read the chapter concerned with that particular area, but read this chapter first to ensure that she is comfortable and relaxed to begin with.

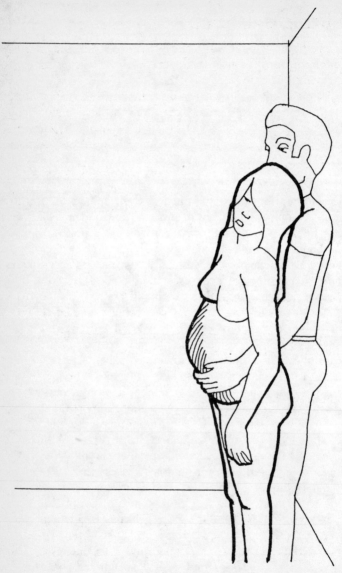

64 Lifting the bump

Lifting the bump

A pregnant woman, especially towards the end of her pregnancy, will welcome this relief from the burden of carrying her baby.

Stand behind her with your arms around her so that your hands rest under the bump slightly to each side of it. She should lean against you resting her head on you. You should lean against a wall or door frame; not against a door. See Drawing 64 opposite.

Lift up her bump gently a little with both hands and hold it for a minute or so. Then gently release. Rest for a few seconds and repeat. Do this several times. Repeat several times a day.

Low back ache

Low back ache is very common in pregnancy. While there may be many causes for it, some simple massage can help bring much relief.

There are five positions for massaging this area. Choose the one one which is most comfortable.

● Lying on her front, using pillows above and below the bump. See drawing 65 below.
● Lying on her side partly face down. Her top arm should

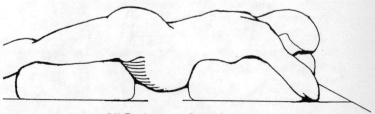

65 Lying on her front

66 Lying partly face down

be in front of her, bottom arm behind her, top knee bent and her bottom knee straight. This is called the recovery position in first aid. Some pillows may be needed around the tummy to make the position comfortable. See Drawing 66 above.

● Sitting on a chair facing its back, with forearms and head leaning on the back of the chair and resting on a pillow. See Drawing 67 opposite.

● Sitting on a stool or a chair at a table. With her legs apart she should lean forwards and rest her head and forearms on the table. See Drawing 68 on page 216.

● Kneeling on the floor resting the head and arms on a chair with knees apart and feet under her bottom. See Drawing 69 on page 217.

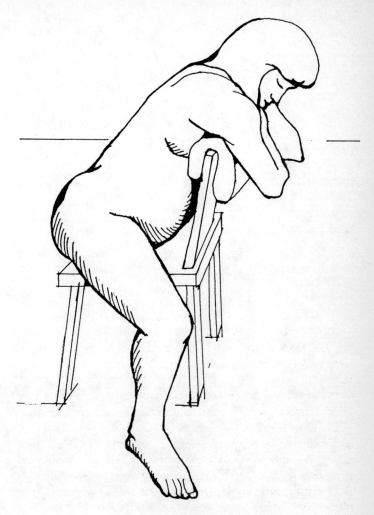

67 Sitting in a chair

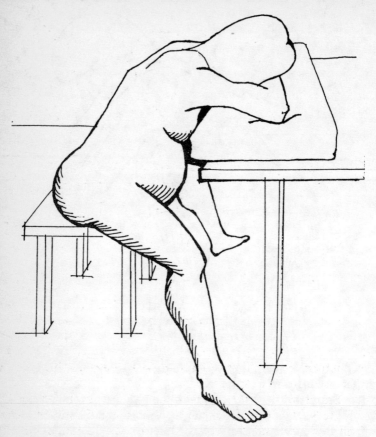

68 Leaning against a table

Stroking the back

Lying on her front or side Since you are going to massage a small area from the low back up to the bra you can use the floor rather than a table if you prefer. Ensure she is comfortable lying on a carpet or duvet with pillows to support her. If she is lying on a table it is important for

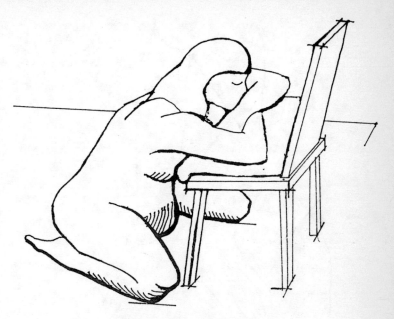

69 Kneeling on the floor

you to make sure that the table is at the right height. This is discussed in chapter 7.

Stand or kneel at her side so that you are level with her buttocks, facing towards her head. Put a small amount of oil in your hands and place them on the bottom of her back, where the buttocks start. Your palms should be resting on her back with your thumbs touching each other over her spine so that your hands are placed either side of the spine. See drawing 70 overleaf.

Leaning onto her back slide your hands up her back. Do not push. Do not apply any pressure with your thumbs onto the spine. They should just rest on it. Apply pressure through leaning on the palms of your hands.

Once you feel you are starting to stretch stop. Do not

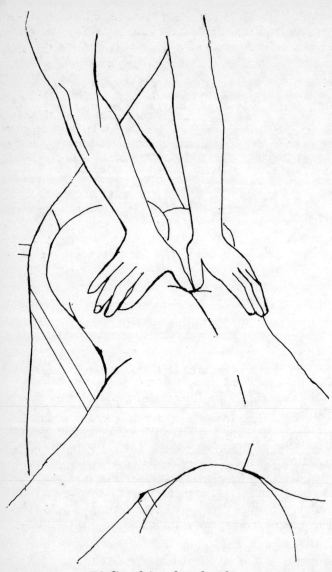

70 Stroking her back

remove your hands but keep them in light contact with her skin and slide them back to the starting point. You have now done one stroke. The next stroke is the same except you should separate your hands by about half an inch.

Repeat this until your hands have reached her sides. Then return to the starting position keeping light hand contact and start again. This time use a little more pressure. Repeat this cycle until you are using a lot of pressure or she feels that you are strong enough. Then reduce your pressure over successive cycles until you are back to the starting pressure.

Sitting or kneeling Massage from above downwards. Stand or kneel at her side facing towards her bottom and place your hands on her back a little below the level of her bra. Your hands should be either side of the spine with the thumbs touching each other over the spine.

Massage with the palms of your hands. Put a small amount of oil on them first. Lean on her back (do not push) and slide your palms down her back towards her buttocks. Do not press the spine with your thumbs. It is more important to massage the lower part of her back than the upper. If you find that you cannot reach the buttocks restart a bit further down the back by altering your position.

Successive strokes should start a little further from the spine until you reach her sides. The cycle should then be repeated with greater pressure. When the pressure is enough reduce it over successive cycles until you are back to the starting pressure. Remember to maintain skin contact while moving your hands from stroke to stroke. This makes the person being massaged feel reassured.

Swollen ankles and feet

Ankles often become swollen in pregnancy especially towards the end of the day. This can be helped by two simple procedures. The first is to relax the ankles and feet while the second is to massage the calves.

There are four positions for massaging this area:

● Sitting in a low chair. Although in general upright chairs are better a low easychair may be more comfortable and relaxing. Experiment with pillows to improve comfort especially in the low back.

● Lying on her back. Make sure this position is tolerable if the pregnancy is well advanced. She may need to be propped up with some pillows under her head, neck and shoulders. She may also need pillows under her low back and knees. Experiment with pillows to make sure she is comfortable.

● Lying on her side partly face down. Her top arm should be in front of her, bottom arm behind her, top knee bent and her bottom knee straight. Some pillows may be needed around the tummy to make the position comfortable. See Drawing 66 on page 214.

● Lying on her front. If the pregnancy is at all advanced this may be uncomfortable. It will help to put pillows above and below the bump so that it is supported without pressure. See Drawing 65 on page 213.

With any of the last three positions you can use a table or the floor. If you use a table the ankles should rest over the end with suitable padding under them. Use blankets or a duvet to make the table comfortable. Refer to chapter 7 to make sure the table is the right height for you.

If using the floor kneel by her feet and rest her ankles on your thigh or a cushion so that they are supported off the ground. You will exert a certain amount of pressure and she will find it uncomfortable if her feet are forceably stretched. Avoid draughts and make sure that the floor is not too hard. Put down a duvet or a few blankets if necessary.

She should take off her shoes, tights, stockings or socks. There is no need for her to remove any more clothes.

Relaxing swollen feet and ankles

Hold the big toe of one foot between the big knuckle and the smaller one above it with your index finger and thumb. With your other hand hold the toe between the nail and the smaller knuckle so that your hands are holding either side of the smaller knuckle.

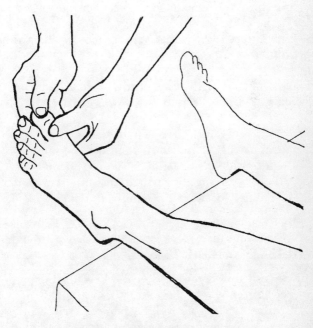

71 Relaxing her toes (1)

Gently, without gripping too hard or being too vigorous, move her toe up and down with your second hand while keeping your first hand still. You are thus alternately bending and straightening this knuckle. See Drawing 71 on the previous page.

Then move both your hands so they are holding either side of the big knuckle, and repeat.

Repeat this for the other toes of both feet. Remember that the smaller toes have three knuckles and not two like the big toe. Deal with each knuckle separately.

Hold the big knuckle on the big toe between the index finger and thumb of one hand and hold the next toe similarly with the other hand. Move one hand up while moving the other hand down in a scissor movement, then repeat the other way round. Do not be too strong or you may hurt. Repeat this with the other toes. See Drawing 72 opposite.

Grasp the foot with one hand and hold the bottom of the leg just above the ankle with your other hand. Firmly but gently, not too strongly, move the foot around. First move it up and down, then side to side, and lastly with a circular movement, first to the left and then to the right. Make quite wide movements but do not be too enthusiastic. If there is the slightest pain or discomfort stop. Repeat with the other foot. See Drawing 73 on page 224.

Massage tired calves

The calves can become swollen and tired during pregnancy especially towards the end. Massaging this area can reduce the swelling as well as being very soothing and relaxing. Massage up the leg away from the ankle but do not use a lot of strength. Avoid any varicose veins,

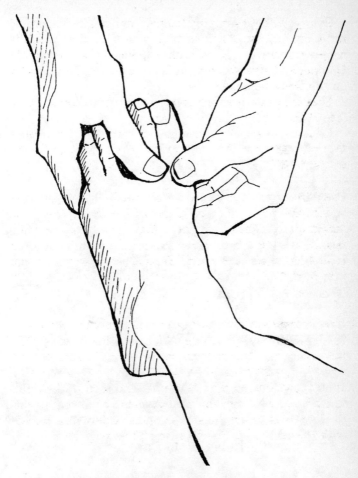

72 Relaxing her toes (2)

especially if they are large. Go around them but not over them.

The calves can be massaged with the pregnant woman lying on her front or her back. If she can lie on her front

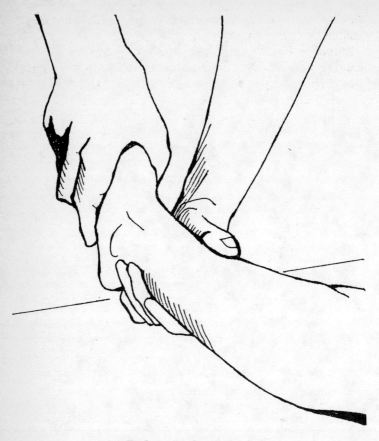

73 Relaxing her ankles

you will be able to give her a better massage than if she has to sit or lie on her back. Massaging with her sitting or lying on her back is described on page 229.

Lying on her front

The pregnant woman should lie on her front in either of

the last two positions described on page 220. Her legs should be slightly apart.

Stand or kneel at her side (it does not matter which side) so you are just below her feet, half facing towards her head.

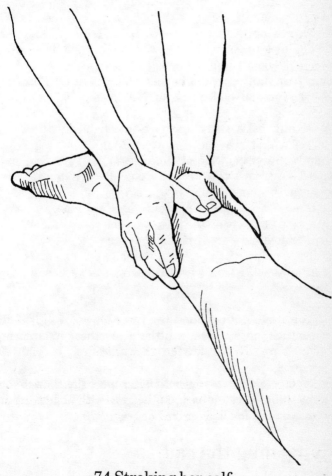

74 Stroking her calf

Put both hands above the ankle near you so your thumbs meet in the middle. Using a small amount of oil on your hands, firmly but gently slide them up towards the back of the knee. Apply pressure with your palms, not your fingers. The pressure should come from leaning your body weight onto your palms and not by pushing. Your fingers should rest on the flesh rather than do any work. See Drawing 74 on the previous page.

The distance you cover towards the knee depends on how tall you are and how long her legs are. If you find you start to overstretch you have gone far enough. Return to where you started keeping light skin contact.

With successive strokes move your hands further apart from each other by half an inch so after a few strokes your hands are either side of the calf. Make sure that each stroke overlaps the previous one. Return to the start position keeping light skin contact.

Repeat with greater pressure. Continue this cycle gradually increasing the pressure each time until either of you feel you are applying enough pressure.

Then reduce the pressure gradually on each cycle until you are back where you started. You have now finished this area.

If you have not reached the knee move towards it and repeat. Stand or kneel a little below the new area and make sure the strokes on the new area overlap the previous area.

If you plan to massage both legs repeat the above on the other calf. Go round to the other side or ask her to turn round so her head is where her feet were.

Kneading the calf

Stand or kneel facing the side of her calf, it does not

matter which side. The closer you are the better. Knead the far sides of both calves from this position.

Use one hand, preferably your strong one (right if you are right handed, left if you are left handed). Rest the other hand on her leg.

Place the heel of your hand with a little oil on it on the centre of her nearer calf just where the achilles tendon disappears and the muscle starts to enlarge. Let your fingers rest on the calf.

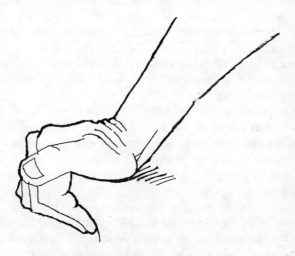

75 Kneading her calf

Keeping your finger tips where they are, move the heel of your hand towards them. Your hand will move away from you towards the far side of the calf and the flesh lying between the heel of your hand and the ends of your fingers will get squeezed. See Drawing 75 above.

The pressure in massage comes from using your body

weight and here the pressure comes from applying your body weight through the heel of your hand. Your fingers apply a resistance to this movement and thus the muscle gets kneaded between them.

Take care not to pull your fingers towards the heel of your hand. If you do you may pinch the calf and you will not be able to apply much pressure. Also ensure your finger tips do not dig into the calf. It is not the actual tips which should be pressing on the calf but the pads at the end of your fingers.

When the heel of your hand has reached your finger ends keep it where it is and stretch out your fingers so that they rest further round her calf. Then repeat the kneading action moving the heel of your hand to your fingers. When you cannot go any further round move your hand back to the middle of the calf, keeping light skin contact.

Move your hand about half a hand width further up the calf and do the same stroke. Continue until you reach the top of the calf, just below the knee.

Return to where you started keeping light skin contact and repeat with greater pressure. Continue to do this, each time increasing the pressure, until eventually either of you feel there is enough pressure. Then gradually reduce the pressure as you built it up until you get back to the initial level.

Both hands Swap hands and knead with your weaker one. When you are happy using your other hand you are ready to use both together. The method of kneading with each hand is the same but they should be used in a co-ordinated manner with your hands alternating.

Start with your hand nearer her head. As it is finishing

its stroke your second hand should come in, nearer her
foot but slightly overlapping the first one. Then as that
hand is finishing its stroke the first hand should restart,
nearer her head and again slightly overlapping the
previous stroke.

It helps if you turn the currently working hand onto its
little finger side as it finishes its stroke. This gives space
for the next hand to start without any loss of contact
between strokes.

If you are massaging both legs do the far side of her
other calf next. Then knead the near side of one or both
legs. To do this go round to her other side or asking her to
turn round so her head is where her feet were. Repeat the
massage as described above.

Sitting or lying on her back

If lying on her front is not comfortable she can lie on her
back or sit in a low chair. Her knee should be bent with
her foot resting on the floor, or table if she is lying on one.
Use one hand to steady her knee. To prevent her foot
sliding, rest one of your knees, or else sit, on the surface in
front of her foot. Drawing 76 overleaf illustrates the
position. The other leg can rest straight out.

Use a kneading stroke If you are massaging her left calf
steady her left knee with your left hand. Place your right
hand with a little oil on the back of her calf just where the
achilles tendon disappears and the muscle starts to
enlarge. The heel of your hand should be on the outside of
the calf with the finger tips resting on the back.

Keep your finger tips where they are and move the
heel of your hand towards them. The flesh lying between
the heel of your hand and the ends of your fingers will get

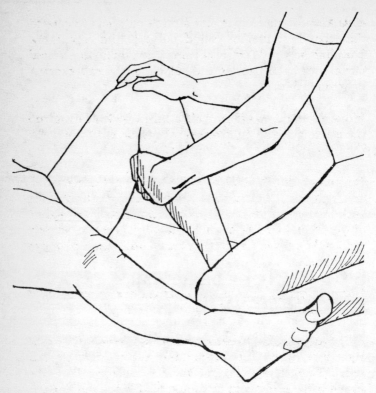

76 Position to massage calf

squeezed. See Drawing 75 on page 227.

Take care not to pull your fingers towards the heel of your hand. If you do you may pinch the calf and will not be able to apply much pressure. Also ensure your finger tips do not dig into the calf. It is not the actual tips which should be pressing on the calf but the pads at the end of your fingers.

When the heel of your hand has reached your finger

ends keep it where it is and stretch out your fingers so that they rest further round her calf and repeat the kneading action. When you cannot go any further round move your hand back to the outside of the calf keeping light skin contact.

Move your hand about half a hand width further up the calf and do the same stroke. Continue until you reach the top of the calf, just below the knee.

Return to where you started keeping light skin contact and repeat with greater pressure. Continue to do this, each time increasing the pressure, until eventually either of you feel there is enough pressure. Then gradually reduce the pressure as you built it up until you get back to the initial level.

Change hands, holding her left knee with your right hand and knead the calf from the inside.

Massage the right calf Hold the right knee with your right hand while you massage the outside with your left hand. Then use your right hand to massage from the inside while using your left hand to stabilise the knee.

Swollen wrists and hands

Wrists can get swollen in pregnancy. An equally good reason for massaging them is the relaxing effect it has on the body as a whole.

The pregnant woman should be lying on her back, or sit in a comfortable chair. Sit, kneel or stand next to her so you can hold her hand comfortably. Avoid bending as your back may start to ache after a little time. She need not remove any clothes but long sleeves should be rolled back to above the elbow.

77 Relaxing her fingers (1)

Lightly hold her index finger between the nail and end
knuckle with your index finger and thumb. With your
other hand hold the same finger between the end knuckle
and next knuckle so that you are gripping either side of
her end knuckle. Gently move your first hand up and
down while keeping the second one still. You are thus
alternately bending and straightening her end knuckle.
Do not be too strong or enthusiastic. Move your hands so
you hold either side of her next knuckle (see Drawing 77)
and repeat, and then again with the big knuckle. Do this
with all four fingers and the thumb of both hands.

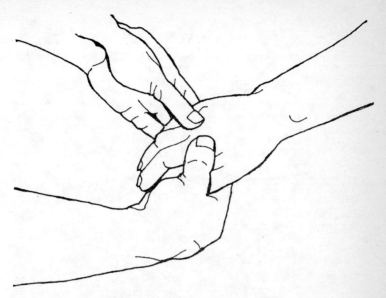

78 Relaxing her fingers (2)

Turn her hand palm downwards With your thumb and index finger hold her middle finger at the big knuckle where her finger joins her hand. Similarly hold her index finger with your other hand. See Drawing 78 above. Gently, firmly and slowly move her middle finger upwards and the index finger downwards by a small amount in a scissors movement. Then reverse the direction. Repeat several times so you are moving her two fingers up and down in opposite directions to each other. Do not grip too tightly and do not move them too far or you will hurt and may cause injury. Repeat this between the other fingers of both hands.

Hold her hand as for a handshake Keeping her wrist still with your other hand, move her hand backwards,

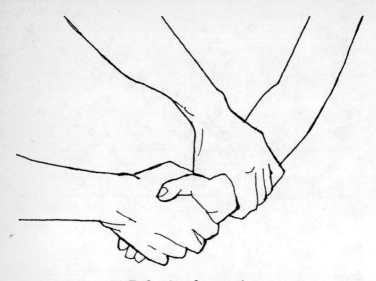

79 Relaxing her wrists

forwards, sideways and then around. See Drawing 79
above. Do not be too strong and never force her hand or
take it further than is comfortable. Encourage her to
relax. If she cannot, make sure you are not gripping too
hard or being too energetic. This should never hurt.

Stroking her forearm

With her in the same position stand, kneel or sit by her
side facing towards her head. Hold her hand with one of
yours, being careful not to grip too tightly.

Place your other hand with a small amount of oil on it
on the side of her forearm just above her wrist. Your
thumb should be on the front of her forearm and your
fingers on the back so that the side of her arm is
sandwiched between them. See Drawing 80.

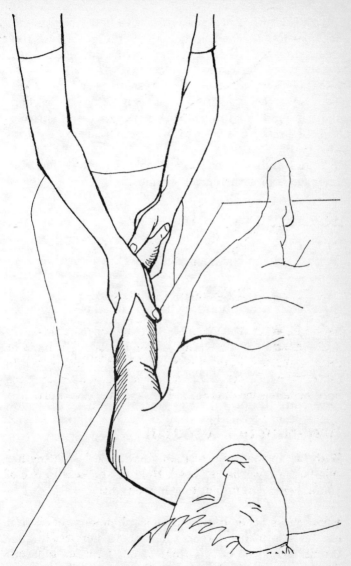

80 Stroking her forearm

Exerting gentle even pressure with both your thumb and index finger slide your hand up her forearm until you reach her elbow. Return to her wrist and repeat with slightly greater pressure.

Repeat this, increasing the pressure each time until either of you feels you are exerting enough pressure. Then gradually ease off the pressure with successive strokes until the pressure is back to the starting level.

Change hands so that you are massaging the other side of her forearm with your other hand.

Kneading her forearm

Start in the same position as you did for stroking the forearm, holding her hand gently but firmly with one of yours.

Place your other hand, with a small amount of oil on your thumb, on the side of her forearm just above her wrist. Your thumb should be on the front of her forearm and your fingers on the back so that the side of her arm is sandwiched between them. See Drawing 80 on page 235.

Slide your thumb towards your fingers Your fingers should stay where they are while your thumb moves towards them so that the flesh gets kneaded between your thumb and fingers. Be careful not to pinch or dig your thumb or fingers in. The kneading action takes place between the pads of the thumb and fingers and not between their tips. See Drawing 81 opposite.

Move your hand up her arm by half an inch keeping light skin contact and repeat. When you have reached her elbow return to the wrist keeping light skin contact.

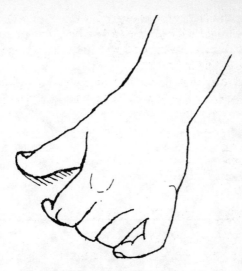

81 Thumb kneading her arm

Repeat with greater pressure Each time you return to her wrist gradually increase the pressure. Continue in this fashion until either of you feel you are applying enough pressure.

Gradually reduce the pressure as you built it up until you are back at the starting pressure.

Change hands and knead the other side of the forearm.

Massage the other arm Go round to her other side. If she is lying down and you cannot, ask her to turn round so her head is where her feet were.

If you want to stroke and then knead her arm do both first on one arm and then the other.

Neck and head aches

Headaches often stem from stiff shoulders and neck. These areas need massage just as much in pregnancy as in other phases of life. The way to massage them has been dealt with in detail in chapters 9 and 10. The only difference here is the position the pregnant woman should sit or lie in. The positions for massaging this area are the same as those for massaging the low back of a pregnant woman. Choose the one which is the most comfortable.

Books

Reflexology, Anna Kay and Don Matchan (Thorsons)
Reflexology today, Doreen Bayly (Thorsons)
Self help for your nerves, Claire Weekes
   (Angus & Robertson)
The stress of life, Hans Selye (McGraw-Hill)
Relief without drugs, Ainslie Meares (Fontana)
Simple relaxation, Laura Mitchell (Murray)
Stress and relaxation, Jane Madders (Macdonald)
Relax and be happy, Jane Madders (Unwin)
Treat your own neck, Robin McKenzie
   (Spinal Publications)
The relaxation response, Herbert Benson
   (Collins/Fount Paperbacks)

Organisations

Relaxation for Living, 29 Burwood Park Road, Walton-on-Thames, Surrey KT12 5LH.
International Stress and Tension Control Society, Priory Hospital, Priory Lane, London SW15 5JJ.

Other Popular Titles

ALLERGY? THINK ABOUT FOOD   SUSAN LEWIS
224 pages. £2.95.

This book explains **how natural foods and additives can cause allergic reactions like asthma, eczema, migraine, hyper-activity, bedwetting, aches and pains and even depression.** *The Daily Telegraph* said: "One of the major problems with many additives is that they are known to cause allergies. If you do have one which you cannot trace, **it would be worth investing in a paperback called ALLERGY? THINK ABOUT FOOD.**"

CRYING BABY HOW TO COPE   PAT GRAY
144 pages. £3.50.

Pat Gray helped start CRY-SIS, the national support group for parents with crying babies. *The Guardian* said: "**Full of tips on the problems of yelling infants including how to help yourself survive.**" Dr Miriam Stoppard says she wished she had had the book when she had her two crying babies.

THE SAVERS & INVESTORS GUIDE
208 pages. £4.50.

David Lewis's popular annual guide to personal investment dispels all the confusion surrounding taxation and savings, investment and pension schemes. The book offers practical and impartial advice to men and women on every form of investment and can help to cut your tax bill, perhaps by hundreds of pounds. Sold over a quarter of a million copies.

ASK YOUR BOOKSHOP FOR COPIES OR USE THE FORM OVERLEAF

Healthy Eating

'Over 300 foods and drinks are analysed by the author, Isabel Skypala, who, as chief dietician at London's Brompton Hospital, has years of experience in nutrition. She very usefully checks what each portion contains by way of calories, protein, fat, fibre, sugar, vitamins and minerals.'
Daily Mail

'It must be the most useful down-to-earth guide I have ever read'
Today

'A simple, explanatory guide to family nutrition'
Katie Boyle, TV Times

'The most sensible book on food I've seen packed with useful tips'
The Star

To: **Wisebuy Publications, 25 West Cottages, London NW6 1RJ**

Please send me _____ copies of BANISH STRESS AND PAIN at £4.95 per copy plus 50p p&p or £9 airmail including p&p.

Please send me _____ copies of HEALTHY EATING at £3.95 per copy plus 50p p&p or £8 airmail including p&p.

Please send me _____ copies of ALLERGY? THINK ABOUT FOOD at £2.95 per copy plus 50p p&p or £6 airmail including p&p.

Please send me _____ copies of CRYING BABY HOW TO COPE at £3.50 per copy plus 50p p&p or £6 airmail including p&p.

Please send me _____ copies of THE SAVERS & INVESTORS GUIDE at £4.50 per copy plus 50p p&p or £8 airmail.

I enclose cheque/PO for £ _____ payable to Wisebuy Publications

Name _____
Block letters please

Address _____

_____

_____ Post code _____